SHARE JESUS WITHOUT FEAR

SHARE JESUS WITHOUT FEAR

WILLIAM FAY

WITH LINDA EVANS SHEPHERD

BROADMAN
& HOLMAN
PUBLISHERS

Nashville, Tennessee

Printed in the United States of America

Published by Broadman & Holman Publishers,
Nashville, Tennessee

Scripture quotations are from the Holy Bible, King James Version.

Note: While all the stories are true, some have been fictionalized to protect the identities and privacy of many wonderful people.

This book is dedicated first to Jesus Christ, who is my Lord and my Savior. Its purpose is to provide freedom and encouragement so you can share your faith and never fail.

Without God placing people in my life to encourage, challenge, and correct me, my life and this material would not be possible. I want to thank my wife, Peg, for her patience as God continues to change me. I also want to thank Paul and Kathie Grant for all they have done to make this ministry possible. My thanks goes out to my friend Keita Andrews, who caught fire after learning how to share his faith and led many to Christ. Plus, I am grateful for the twenty-five thousand or so of you with whom I have had the privilege of sharing my faith one on one, many of whom prayed to receive Jesus Christ.

I am grateful to Gordon Lewis, professor of systematic theology at Denver Seminary, for giving me a firm theological foundation so I could be confident in the sovereign work of God. I also appreciate my good friend Tom Weins, who always had the ability to be there with the right help or phone call. A special thanks to all of the pastors who serve Christ faithfully. I see you at work when I visit your churches. I pray for you, honor you, and have the deepest respect for your obedience to follow your call for Jesus Christ.

— William Fay

I thank God for this work. Someday, when we are on the other side, it will be a joy to meet all those who were touched by this book.

— Linda Evans Shepherd

CONTENTS

Chapter 1 YOU CAN'T FAIL

My resume spelled *p-o-w-e-r*. I was the president and CEO of a multimillion-dollar international corporation, I had ties with the mob, and I owned one of the larger houses of prostitution in the United States. I was involved in racketeering, bookmaking, and gambling. I had a gold Rolex, chauffeured limo, money, my fourth wife, *and* trophies from my many racquetball championships. I felt I had everything the world said spelled *success*. And I mocked anyone who dared share his faith in God with me.

One morning, I went to my athletic club looking for someone to annihilate on the racquetball court. As I looked through the little window in the door, I saw a man on the court who appeared to be a Jew. Brazenly, I pushed open the door and demanded, "What are you doing here on Yom Kippur? Why aren't you out doing whatever you Jews do on holidays?"

Paul Grant replied, "I am also a Christian. Yom Kippur is the day Jews ask God to forgive them of their sins for another year. I don't have to do that because I've already received forgiveness through Jesus, the Messiah."

"Oh, please, give me a break," I sneered.

For months afterward, Dr. Grant would stand by his locker while I asked questions, deliberately trying to make him late for his patients. I thought, *What a stupid fool. How can this idiot sit here and let me do this to him?*

It wasn't until a year and a half later, when my house of prostitution was raided, that I ever took him seriously. In the midst of hundreds of phone calls from men, either worried about where the girls were or concerned their names would be found in my records, only Dr. Grant called to ask, "Are you OK?"

That was the first time in my forty years anyone had ever asked me that question. I was so struck by his concern that when he invited me to go to church with him and his wife, Kathie, I accepted.

Still I didn't make it easy for him. Once in church, I sat on the back row. When the attendant tried to pin a rose on me, I threw it like a Frisbee. Later, when the Grants took me to their home, I heard my first Christian testimony from Kathie.

Kathie is the kind of radiant woman who looks as though she'd never had a zit. I stared at her in disbelief as she told her story about how she had been abused as a child and how she had been the mistress to an oil baron in Indonesia. I figured she'd concocted this story as a way to hook me into some sort of cult, which she called Christianity. But the funny thing is, even though I rejected her testimony that day, I can still tell you the dress she wore. I can still remember the teapot from which she poured. Yet I left their house saying, "That's fine for you, but I don't need that junk in my life."

(My complete testimony follows in appendix 4.)

Did They Fail?

Through the years, many people came into my life to share their faith, but I would not receive it. I sent these people away, discouraged, because I either insulted them, antagonized them, or persecuted them. And if they walked away from me believing they had failed, they believed a lie. For I never forgot the name, the face, the person, or the words of anyone who ever told me about Jesus.

God is sovereign! If he can take somebody like me and change him, he can take anybody in your life and change him as well. But be aware: you are *not* responsible for causing a person's heart to turn toward God. Jesus said, "No man can come to me, except the Father which hath sent me draw him" (John 6:44). It is God who draws people to himself, not you. But even so, you do not want to miss God-ordained opportunities to share your faith with others, or you also miss opportunities to experience the good things God had planned for you. Philemon, verse 6, says, "That the communication of thy faith may become effectual by the acknowledging of every good thing which is in you in Christ Jesus."

You see, success is sharing your faith and living your life for Jesus Christ. It has nothing whatsoever to do with bringing anyone to the Lord. It has everything to do with obedience.

Even if you do not have the privilege to see someone respond the first time you share your faith, you have not failed, because you were obedient.

Chapter 2
CATCH THE VISION

One night I had a dream. A woman clutched a little girl, struggling to hold her child's head above the water. Nearby, a wave plunged a man into its salty depths. He choked for air as he thrashed his arms against a ceiling of water. All around, the ocean churned with drowning people, gasping for air and desperately trying to push their heads above the surface. Their screams were doused by the roar of the relentless waves. Their cries caught the wind, but only in vain. They were alone in their terror, with no help in sight.

Then a huge rock appeared, and a voice called into the darkness. People began crawling up the rock's craggy sides to safety.

But when they got to safety, something happened that drove me almost goofy. The people who emerged from the waves got busy. They got involved in building rock gardens, rock lives, rock jobs, listening to their rock music, and going to rock meetings where they talked about the people who were still drowning in the ocean. But nobody went back to the water's edge to help.

Have you ever tried to run or yell in a dream? In my dreams, I can do neither. Yet I tried to run; I tried to yell at the top of my lungs, "How could you have forgotten you were once in the sea?"

As I watched the "saved" scurry about their rock work and as I listened to their rock talk, I realized the rock was the cross of Calvary. The voice they heard was Jesus, calling by the power of the Holy Spirit, inviting them to come join him. He's never high up on the rock where it's safe; he's calling from the ocean's edge, where the dead, the diseased, and the lost are found, and as you might recall, that's where he found you.

Did you know that as few as 5 to 10 percent of the people in an average church have shared their faith in the past year? That means 90 percent of us have chosen the sin of silence. Just like in my dream, those who were drowning have gotten so busy and involved with the safety of "The Rock," they've forgotten to reach out to those who are still drowning.

The Sin of Silence

Debate has flourished about which of the wounds inflicted on Jesus actually caused his death. Among the many wounds he received were lacerations, punctures, abrasions, and contusions. In a sense we can say that none of these killed Jesus. The wound that killed him was silence. No one spoke up for him.

When Jesus was arrested by the Roman soldiers, his loyal disciple, Peter, did not run away but followed at a safe, silent distance as Jesus was marched to the high priest's house. The soldiers took Jesus inside, and Peter joined a group of people warming themselves by a fire. Several people in the crowd recognized Peter as one of Jesus' followers. They questioned him. "Weren't you with Jesus?" But Peter denied it. "Sorry, I don't know him."

Before morning, before the first crow of the rooster, Peter had denied Christ three times. As we read this account, we shake our heads saying, "I'm glad I never did that."

And though most of us have never said, "I don't know him," we've still found a way to deny him. We deny Jesus by never opening our mouths. We deny him with our silence.

We should be excited about sharing our faith. We are living in a time when biblical prophesies are being fulfilled right and left. Yet most of us remain silent.

In the meantime, one hundred thousand churches will close their doors this decade. Why? Because those church members chose the sin of silence.

Watch out for the signs of a dying Christian life. Ask yourself, *Am I sharing my faith? Do I have only Christian friends? Do I hang around the dead, the diseased, and the lost?* If you and the members of your church have forsaken your duty to reach back into the world, I can promise you your church will start to divide, to backbite, and to fight over nonessential Christian issues like hymnal selection and carpet colors. You will become keepers of a Christian aquarium instead of fishers of men. Your church will be on the way to spiritual death. In fact, I can prophesy to any church or to any believer without fear of being in error that if you choose not to evangelize, individually or collectively, your church will fossilize.

Perhaps we have forgotten what happens to those who have not been born again. Before I made my commitment to follow Christ, I lived what I now call the "lie of the middle."

Somehow I believed I wasn't that bad, that I was in the "middle" and therefore deserved to go to heaven. That was a lie. The Bible states that either God is your father or Satan is your father. Either you are in a relationship with Christ, or you're not; either you are born again, or you're not. You are either God's child, or you are God's enemy; you are either storing up wrath, or you are storing up mercy; you are either heaven-bound, or you are hell-bound. No one is in the middle. No one is "almost there." Those who have chosen to reject Christ are *condemned*. It is *wrong* to believe a loving God will *not* send unbelievers to hell.

Think of the cross, where Christ laid himself down and bore our sins. This act demonstrates the unbelievable love of God. But what about the justice of God? When Christ, the spotless Lamb of God, became the bearer of the sins of the world on the cross, he cried out, "My God, my God, why hast thou forsaken me?" (Matt. 27:46). He said, "I am counted with them that go down into the pit: I am as a man that hath no strength: Free among the dead, . . . whom thou rememberest no more" (Ps. 88:4–5).

Scripture makes it clear that God turned his back on Jesus Christ. He heaped all of his waves of wrath on his own spotless Son. Why? Because a holy God cannot look at sin, whether it is committed by you or placed on his only Son.

We must quit believing the lie that you or anyone you know who is not born again is not damned. We must refuse to believe God will allow our unbelieving friends to bypass hell and join us in heaven.

There are only two kinds of people reading this book:

1. Those who talk *about* the lost.
2. Those who talk *to* the lost.

My concern is not who you are now. My concern is who you will become after reading this simple approach to evangelism. Perhaps you have been a member of the first group. My hope is that by the time you have finished this book, you will have joined the second group. But, still, some of those in the second group are only willing to throw hints, instead of life preservers, to those drowning in the sea.

Many Christians tell people they love the Lord. They offer hugs and tell people they'll pray for them, yet they only share hints of gospel truth. Sometimes they put those silver fish and "Honk If You Love Jesus" bumper stickers on the back of their cars. And if they are made of braver stuff, they go to football games and hold up posters with the words "John 3:16" painted in large red letters.

These Christians don't share enough information to allow the Holy Spirit to effect a heart change. They fail to tell their friends how to go from the state of death to the state of life!

Were you ever really hungry at a sweet hostess's home? As your stomach growled louder, you were relieved to notice a lace-covered table in the corner. The table bore an elegant silver platter covered with microscopic sandwiches. You smiled and walked across the plush carpet to stand beside this exquisite table. But once there, you discovered that no matter how long you sampled the wares off the lovely platter, you simply couldn't get filled.

The same principle applies to those Christians who offer their friends only spiritual tidbits. Their friends will go away hungry, wishing to be filled with life.

These same Christians say, "Bill, I go to church, I live a good Christian life, but I never share my faith."

But the problem is, if you aren't sharing your faith, you are *not* living a good Christian life. Romans 10:14 says, "How then shall they call on him in whom they have not believed? and how shall they believe in him of whom they have not heard?"

We must realize if we don't explain our faith, our friends may never understand it and, therefore, never have an opportunity to be led by the Holy Spirit to believe it.

Marnie, a young mother of two, prayed God would make her sensitive to those who were lost. Later, she visited an elderly friend in the hospital.

"I wanted to share my faith with Jim, but I didn't know what to say. All I could think of was to tell him God loved him. He was receptive, and I wanted to say more, but I was at a total loss for words.

"When Jim was feeling better, he called me on the phone. As he was hanging up, he said, 'Oh, be sure to tell God hi for me.'

"That got to me. I decided it was time to learn how to share my faith. I went through Bill's material, marked my Sharing Bible/New Testament, then went to see Jim. Although he still had questions, he was so receptive to what I shared. I had no idea it could be so easy. Now I am looking for more opportunities to witness."

Some Christians say, "Yep, witnessing can happen through my pastor, Bill Fay, or a TV evangelist, but God can't do that through me." If this is how you feel, then you forget that "God hath chosen the foolish things of the world to confound the wise" (1 Cor. 1:27).

But if you, like Marnie, share the gospel with a friend, you can release the power to change that person, and perhaps the power to change history.

If you need proof of this truth, look in the mirror, because when you heard the gospel, your life changed. If your life has *not* changed, then you've never met him. It is time you did! Please turn to the review at the end of chapter 6 to find out how your life can be changed.

Chain Reaction

When we seize opportunities, they can grow into chain reactions. One afternoon I visited one of my favorite restaurants, the Black-Eyed Pea. After the lunch rush was over, I asked the waitress, "Where are you from?"

"Ohio," she responded.

"How did you get from Ohio to Denver?"

She sounded wistful. "I came to get married."

I looked into her sad eyes. "Didn't happen?"

She hung her head. "No."

I leaned forward. "If you're interested, I have a solution for your pain."

She looked up. "Can I bring a friend?"

I said, "No problem."

And so we met in downtown Denver, at the Sixteenth Street Mall, the next day at high noon. With the lunch crowd's chatter and clinking glasses, it was probably the worst location we could have picked.

Yet despite the chaos around us, these two women, with many tears, gave their hearts and lives to Christ.

Then the friend looked at her watch.

I asked, "Did I keep you too long?"

She said, "No, Bill. I gotta go back to my office and tell everybody they can get their sins forgiven, just like I did."

There is a problem in the church today; it is subtle, but it is there. It is people like us telling people like her, "Wait! Hold it! You don't know enough. You haven't been to the beginner's class. You don't even have a Bible, and you haven't learned to pray! You can't share your faith with someone. You're not ready!"

But what about the woman at the well? After she heard the good news, she ran into town to tell her friends. So did this lady. Twenty minutes later, I got a phone call from a woman in her office who said, "Would you come back down and meet with me?"

I did. I found out that she had, for thirteen months, been active in adultery. The last two months, she had been living away from her own husband.

The next thing I knew, she gave her life to Christ. Two days later, I heard from her husband. He called me and said, "Something's happened to my wife. She came home. She asked me to forgive her. Bill, whatever's happened to her? I want it to happen to me."

He came, he heard, and he received. The next Sunday, he sat in the front row of the church with his wife, giving God credit for their restored marriage.

Two weeks later, I got a call from the adulterer. He called to find out how his former lover could have possibly left him.

I invited him down for a chat. He came, he heard, but to my frustration, he didn't receive. But you know what? He's not my problem. I had the privilege of choosing obedience to share the gospel of Jesus Christ. I didn't fail; I obeyed, and that was success.

Don't Trade Tidbits for Truth

Success is not forcing someone to make a commitment to follow Christ. And often when I share my faith, the person with whom I've shared may not *seem* to respond.

When Dr. Grant and his wife, Kathie, first shared the gospel with me, I rejected it. But I did not forget it. Their work was an important factor in my eventual decision a year and a half later.

Nonbelievers must hear the gospel an average of 7.6 times before they receive it. So if anyone walks away from you when you share the gospel with him, remember: the Word of God never returns void. Maybe the person you shared with has never heard it before. Maybe this is only the second time he has ever heard it, or maybe this is his 6.6th time. Your obedience to share may bring this person to a turning point. That is why we must walk by faith and not by sight. So if a woman walks away from a gospel presentation, that presentation may still be the seed that eventually produces fruit. She may count the encounter as the turning point to following Christ.

What kind of encounters does the Holy Spirit use most often to produce fruit? He uses a witness whose heart is motivated by love. A survey from the Institute of American Church Growth showed that 75 to 90 percent of new believers come to Christ through a friend or acquaintance who explains the good news on a one-to-one basis. Only 17 percent of all conversions come through what is called an "event"—a pastor giving his Sunday morning message, a Billy Graham crusade, or a Friendship Sunday. Yet, most churches devote the majority of their time, energy, and money to these kinds of events.

Can you imagine a businessman investing the majority of his resources in opportunities he knew would produce the least profits? Of course not. He would try to concentrate his resources on profitable opportunities. We need to follow his example when it comes to investing our time and resources into sharing our faith. As we see the importance of sharing our faith on a one-to-one basis, we must be ready to offer more than mere tidbits of truth. We can't just say to someone, "God loves you," or "I'll pray for you," or "I go to church." We must be prepared to share the whole gospel. "Be ready always to give an answer to every man that asketh you a reason of the hope that is in you with meekness and fear" (1 Pet. 3:15).

This book will encourage you to realize that when you share your faith, you can't fail. It will show you a fresh and dynamic way you can use to tenderly and fearlessly confront people with the gospel of Jesus Christ. You can feel like a success, knowing God has a special place in his heart for people who are obedient to his Word.

A forty-year-old computer programmer from Boulder, Colorado, agrees. Wayne says, "The witnessing technique Bill teaches has helped me live a lifestyle of sharing my faith naturally. When I use the questions Bill recommends, my friends not only know I care about their needs, they know I care about their deepest need: their relationship with God. They know I will listen to what they are saying. They need that. Then, because I have listened, I am granted the opportunity to use the power of Scripture to show truth in a nonthreatening way."

Are you, like Wayne, willing to be obedient to Jesus' call to share your faith? Perhaps it is time to leave the safety of the rock fortress and venture to the ocean's edge. Perhaps it is time to use his words of truth as life preservers for those who could be rescued from the depths of sin. Jesus is already standing on the shore, and he is calling you to join him in his work. The question remains: will you go?

Since you are a member of the Gideons International and are reading this book, you have likely developed a certain burden for the salvation of lost souls. The vision is clearly stated in article 2 of our constitution: "The object of the Gideons is to win men, women, boys and girls to the Lord Jesus Christ."

Many tools are available for your use, such as this book (*Share Jesus Without Fear*), the Personal Worker's Testament (PWT), tracts, the "Soul Winning Made Easy" booklet, Scripture Memory Courses, and the Daily Bible Reading Calendar. All designed to make you more effective in daily personal witnessing. Take advantage of these materials and read on. You will not only catch the vision, but you will be used of God in leading others to Christ.

Chapter 3
OVERCOME YOUR FEAR

One day, I had a layover at an airport, so I went to the Red Carpet room to wait for my flight. While I was there, I saw Mohammed Ali, sitting at a table with a briefcase full of tracts about the Moslem faith.

I stopped to visit, and he gave me a couple of his pamphlets. Because of his illness, Parkinson's disease, it took a long time for him to sign his name at the bottom.

As I watched him, I thought, *Here is a man, giving his all with what little physical and mental abilities he has left, to share a lie. Yet too many Christians sit back, too afraid to share the truth.*

Is It Your Job?

God has called each of us to share our faith, in obedience. He has called each of us to evangelize. If one of your excuses for not sharing your faith is, "I don't have the *gift* of evangelism," then you need to examine Scripture. You will find the command of the Great Commission: to evangelize, to encourage evangelism, and to urge evangelism.

I like to explain it this way: I don't have the overt *gift* of giving; it's not a supernatural gift God has given me. Yet I'm *required* to give. I don't have the supernatural *gift* of mercy. Yet I'm *required* to be merciful. In my role as a volunteer police chaplain, it is sometimes my job to hold a mother whose child has died of SIDS. Sometimes I find myself on a murder scene, where I try to comfort the survivors of a horrible tragedy. And even though I hate to visit hospitals, my work takes me to bedsides where I hold the hand of assault victims. And because I am not *naturally* merciful, I have to depend on God to *supernaturally* release his mercy through me.

We all must evangelize through the power of the Holy Spirit. The apostle Paul wrote, "I can do all things through Christ which strengtheneth me" (Phil. 4:13). This means that God has given us the strength to share our faith, despite our lack of gifts, talents, and abilities. For Paul said in Ephesians 1:18–20, "The eyes of your understanding being enlightened; that ye may know . . . what is the exceeding greatness of his power to us-ward who believe, according to the working of his mighty power, Which he wrought in Christ, when he raised him from the dead, and set him at his own right hand in the heavenly places."

This means we have the same power that raised Jesus from the dead, living in us, so we lack nothing to get the job done.

The Bible makes it clear that there is the *office* of the evangelist, as well as the *office* of pastor and teacher as found in Ephesians 4:11–13: "And he gave some . . . evangelists; and some, pastors and teachers; For the perfecting of the saints, for the work of the ministry, for the edifying of the body of Christ: Till we all come in the unity of the faith, and of the knowledge of the Son of God, unto a perfect man, unto the measure of the stature of the fulness of Christ."

From this Scripture, we can see God has called the pastor, the teacher, and the evangelist to prepare and to equip the body for works of service.

Because God has called the evangelist to equip the body of Christ, I can exercise my office by equipping you to share your faith. As an evangelist, I must tell you that just because evangelism might be difficult for you, you do not have an excuse to ignore it. When you are obedient in sharing your faith, you are giving God an opportunity to work *through* you, perhaps even *despite* you. Jesus told us, *"Go!"* This was not an option; it was a command!

So why do we struggle to share our faith? Why are we so afraid? Let's take a look at the top six fears that keep people from sharing their faith, and let's discover how to overcome them.

Note: An important tool in the Gideon ministry is the Personal Worker's Testament, referred to hereafter as simply the PWT. The PWT contains the "Where to Find Help" section in the front and the plan of salvation in the back inside cover. These tools are invaluable in overcoming the fear of personal witnessing.

1. I'm afraid of being rejected.

There is no stronger pain than the pain of rejection. At least, that's how Bob saw it. His fear of rejection was so acute he cut himself off from all ties with his daughter. He hadn't seen Carry since he'd divorced her mother, over fifteen years earlier. He was afraid to contact Carry because he felt she would reject the very sight of him. So he stayed away, never giving her the chance to slam the door in his face.

How can a man like Bob conquer the fear of rejection? How can a man like Bob ever succeed with evangelism?

Just what is successful evangelism? For one thing, it is not a contest. As we've discussed, success is sharing your faith and living your life for Jesus Christ. It has nothing whatsoever to do with bringing anyone to the Lord.

We need to get away from the "win them" mentality. People do not put their faith in Christ because we force them to believe. They put their faith in Christ because God uses us to point out the truth. If we have "won" someone to Christ, then he or she is probably not saved. It is said that D. L. Moody, the evangelist, was riding on a train after a crusade. An old drunk came up to him and said, "You know, Mr. Moody, I'm one of your converts."

Mr. Moody looked him right in the eye and said, "Son, I'm afraid you are one of mine, because you are obviously not a convert of Christ's."[1] Moody understood the difference.

When people reject your message, it is not you they reject; they are rejecting Jesus and God's Word. Therefore, you didn't fail in your obedience. Even if the way you share the message is tactless or unloving, God can use it. What he can't use is your sin of silence.

I've seen some strange ways people share their faith. For example, a youth director and his teens bought a casket. A teen in "dead guy" makeup climbed inside. The group took the casket with the dead guy down to Main Street. There they hauled the casket up and down the street while a tape player blared New Orleans revelry music. As a crowd gathered, the teens slipped the lid off the casket, revealing the "body," his eyes closed and his hands folded across his chest. Then the pretend pastor began a eulogy. "This here is nice, old John. He liked to fish and he loved to read his books."

Suddenly the dead guy's eyes popped open, and he jumped out of the casket. He pointed at the pastor, shouting, "You never told me I had to be born again to enter the kingdom of heaven. You never shared your faith with me. You never gave me the chance to make a decision to follow Christ! Now I'm on my way to hell because of you."

While the people who watched this drama unfold stared in shock, the teens began to pass out tracts and to witness. Several members of the audience made commitments to follow Christ.

Personally, I wouldn't be caught dead masquerading as a corpse. However, God used even this outrageous approach because these teens were faithful in sharing the good news.

Let's suppose you went out today and tried to share your faith with the first person you saw, and he or she told you to go away. Have you failed? No way. You've chosen obedience to the gospel. Let's imagine the next day, a friend of yours shared his faith with the first person he saw, and this person not only responded to the gospel but became a replacement for Billy Graham. Can your friend take credit for that? Absolutely not.

There is no success, no failure, in God's kingdom when people choose obedience. In fact, this is the one area of your Christian life you ultimately cannot botch. Even if you share stupidly, unlovingly, or with poor timing, our heavenly Father can use it. What he can't use is your silence.

The apostle Paul shared his faith "in weakness, and in fear, and in much trembling" (1 Cor. 2:3). Yet Paul made a difference because he *went,* and God used him. And it couldn't have been a lot of fun to be beaten, pelted with stones, shipwrecked, snake-bitten, and lowered naked into a pit. But in spite of the personal cost Paul paid, he went. And every time he went, God enabled him with the Holy Spirit. Despite the difficulties, Paul was able to count his suffering as joy.

That's what we want for our Christian lives. Even as the stones are thrown, even when the stones hurt, somehow God turns our pain to joy.

How can we find that joy of sharing our faith when we are *so* afraid of rejection? Let's take another look at Bob, the father who had been estranged from his daughter for fifteen years. When Bob heard me preach on the sin of silence, he made a decision. He decided before he left the church that he would go to the church office and phone his daughter. Minutes after the service, he called Carry and asked her to forgive him. Then he began to tell her how God had changed his life.

The next evening, Bob and Carry met, and after years of being separated because of the fear of rejection, Bob again asked Carry for forgiveness and led his daughter to Christ. *That* is joy!

Not everyone who shares his faith sees a positive response. For example, an introverted young man made the decision to share his faith with a coworker. He relates, "I shared my faith with Sara, but she did not make a commitment to follow Christ. Yet I am thrilled because I was able to take her through the process of sharing my faith. I never realized it could be so easy."

Another woman shared her faith with a family member who responded with an abrupt, "No way."

Later, Lauren said, "That's OK. I'll chalk that share time up as number one. I'm not finished. If it takes an average 7.6 times for a person to hear the gospel before it changes his life, then I've just begun. I've got one down, and 6.6 more times to go!"

The PWT, when properly presented, lessens the possibility of rejection. When unbelievers are confronted with God's Word, they instantly feel condemnation. The devil has made sure of this for centuries. The "Where to Find Help" section, in the front of the PWT, reduces this feeling by showing them that the Bible was written to help them, not condemn them.

2. I'm afraid of what my friends will think.

Martha, a woman in her early sixties, approached me one evening after a seminar.

"My husband and children aren't saved," Martha said with tears running down her cheeks. "I've never had the courage to explain the gospel to them. I was always worried about what they would think!"

Is that why you stay silent—because you are worried about what your friends will think? Well, let me ask, what do they think of you now?

Either you can share your faith, or you can say nothing and in your silence love your friends into hell.

Some people say, "I'm afraid my friends will persecute me if I share."

Jesus promised us nothing less. He said, "If they have persecuted me, they will also persecute you" (John 15:20).

Yet this is not all bad news. Matthew 5:10–12 promises a double blessing when we are persecuted: "Blessed are they which are persecuted for righteousness' sake: for theirs is the kingdom of heaven. Blessed are ye, when men shall revile you, and persecute you, and shall say all manner of evil against you falsely, for my sake. Rejoice, and be exceeding glad: for great is your reward in heaven."

How many of your friends know you are a Christian but don't understand the gospel? The reason many of your friends have not received the gospel is because they are waiting for you to explain it to them.

Kristine was surprised to find this to be true. She had known Joel for twenty years. He knew she was a Christian, yet she had never explained the gospel to him. After hearing a presentation on how to share her faith, she decided she would contact Joel and present the gospel, even though she felt it would mean the end of their friendship.

A few days later, when he was sitting on her sofa, she said, "Joel, all these years, you have always known where I am spiritually. But how about you? Where are you?"

Because Kristine was finally able to ask, Joel opened up to her. Kristine presented the gospel to him, and he submitted his life to the Lord.

I am also happy to say that Martha, the older woman who had never shared her faith with her family, also caught the vision. Later that night, after the seminar, she told me, "Tonight I have found the courage and the freedom to tell my family about Jesus, and the *first* person I am going to share him with is going to be my husband!"

Although Martha and Albert had never discussed spiritual matters, she went home and asked the five opening questions. When she finished the questions, he gave her permission to show him the Scriptures. When he understood he needed to ask Jesus into his life to forgive his sins, he made the commitment joyfully. The following week, Martha and Albert went to each of their children and shared their faith with them. Their sons and daughter also accepted Christ as their Savior.

After that, Albert took time off work, and he and Martha visited in other states where they had the privilege of sharing their faith and leading their loved ones to Jesus.

3. I don't think I can share with my coworkers.

Ray, a pastor of a small church in Arizona and former boxing professional, also moonlighted in construction work. He had a reputation before he became a Christian for barroom brawls. In and out of the ring, he was always a winner. His coworkers not only teased and mocked Ray for his faith, they ridiculed God. Ray said, "It took every ounce of my being to not take care of these mockers the way I would have before I became a Christian."

But instead of reacting, he simply prayed for his coworkers and cautioned them to show respect toward God.

One day, Ray and two coworkers were working on the top of a scaffold, painting. An explosion suddenly rocked the air, knocking everyone, except Ray, off the scaffold. His two coworkers plummeted into a wall of flames. Ray jumped down and wrapped one man in his own clothing, trying to stop the fire. As he held the man in his arms, the mocker said, "You warned me, didn't you?"

And Ray said, "Yes, I did."

The man gave his life to the Lord on the spot. That night, Ray went to visit the other victim in the hospital. This man was so impressed by Ray's servant spirit he asked, "How can you possibly love me like this after the way I've treated you?"

A week later, the second burn victim released from the hospital invited Ray to his home and gave his life to Jesus Christ. Both men now attend Ray's church.

Is it important to share your faith with your coworkers? Yes. After all, God has put them in your path, perhaps for that very reason. One woman who attended my seminars said, "Now that I know how to share my faith, I have a new confidence. I am no longer ashamed of who I am at work. I realize when I am persecuted for my faith, I am doubly blessed. And God has given me the opportunity to be a living witness. I especially liked the quote you gave from Saint Francis of Assisi: 'Preach the gospel at all times and if necessary, use words.'"

I do not believe you should take time to present the gospel at work. Yes, it is OK to qualify by asking the first five "Share Jesus Questions," which I will present to you in chapter 4. These five questions will only take a matter of moments to ask. So feel free to test the waters to see if a coworker is open to the gospel. If he is, invite him to lunch, to your home, or to your church in order to present the gospel.

There can always be an exception to my "no-share" rule, especially when you are sharing with your boss. For example, Lois had worked as Randal's assistant for a number of years. She said, "He knew I was a Christian and used to tease me about my faith. In fact, one Monday, he asked, 'Did you go and do that church stuff again?'

"And I asked, 'What do you mean by church stuff?'

"He said, 'Well, what is it that you guys do?'"

Lois said, "Let me show you what I learned Sunday night."

She sat down and asked him the five "Share Jesus Questions" she had learned from my seminar, then took him through the verses of Scripture. Right there, Randal gave his life to the Lord. She said, "My husband now disciples Randal, and Randal and I pray together every day before we start work."

4. I don't know enough.

Do you sometimes feel you don't know enough to share your faith? Imagine you had to share your faith with a man like Nate who tests in the upper one percentile in intelligence and reads 1,250 words a minute with total recall.

Imagine this man, so bright that he not only scored one of the highest scores on the Mensa test, a test for geniuses, but found an error in the test while he was taking it.

Nate was a hard case. He had been an atheist for twenty years, and his hobby was tearing apart religions. What kind of person do you think God sent into Nate's life? A fellow genius? A Nobel Prize winner? Josh McDowell?

No, God sent John, a Blackfoot Indian with a twelfth-grade education.

Nate was in the armed services and riding a bus with John. Other soldiers kept throwing John's Bible out of the window to tease him. John would patiently get off the bus and retrieve it, without complaining.

Nate asked him, "Why do you let those clowns do that to you?"

John replied, "Sir, I am a Christian."

Up until this point, Nate had never attacked the Christian faith. He had successfully shredded every other religion. Yet Christianity had stumped him. So he decided he would challenge this simple man of faith.

Nate asked, "Do you mean to tell me you believe somebody got vomited out of the mouth of a whale?"

This simple man of faith said, "Yes, sir."

Nate asked, "Why?"

John answered, "My Bible tells me so."

No matter what question Nate threw at John, John replied with either a yes or no, followed by, "My Bible tells me so."

Nate's great mind could not shake John's faith, and that shook him. That night, Nate went home and borrowed a Bible from a neighbor. He read it through over the weekend.

A verse in Job 5:8–9 struck Nate's heart: "I would seek unto God, and unto God would I commit my cause: Which doeth great things and unsearchable; marvellous things without number."

Nate could not ignore this truth, and it transformed his life. Now Nate is one of the best defenders of the Christian faith I have ever known. How did this happen? Because John, a simple man of faith with a twelfth-grade education, believed a verse, "Not by might, nor by power, but by my spirit, saith the LORD of hosts" (Zech. 4:6).

I find the excuse that "I don't know enough" usually comes from someone who has been a Christian for ten years or more. When I meet someone who tells me this, I like to tease him by saying, "The problem is you have been sitting around accumulating information for so long you're spiritually constipated. You need to get rid of some of this information!"

One advantage of the PWT is the "Where to Find Help" section in the front. Often the unbeliever's questions, pressing needs, or life problems, are addressed in this section. You can then point to areas of help during the conversation and God's Word will answer those questions, or perhaps speak to a deep need in their life. You should spend some time familiarizing yourself with the "Helps" available in this section. This will help you overcome the fear of not having all the answers.

5. I'm afraid of losing my friends and relatives.

I was visiting a ranch when Philip, a businessman who owned a chain of hardware stores, asked me about God.

When I sat down to share the gospel with him, he pulled out a yellow pad and pen to take notes.

When I finished, Philip had written only two or three sentences. He looked up at me and stated, "It's too simple."

I asked, "Why?"

Philip switched and asked, "What is God going to do with all my businesses?"

Since I did not know if God was going to bless Philip or bust him, I activated the "Why Principle," and asked, "Philip, why? What about your businesses?"

He switched again and asked, "What about my mother?"

I knew we had hit the core issue. He went on to tell me that his mother was of a religious denomination that did not make faith in Christ personal. She had told him she would disown him if he ever accepted Christ as his Savior.

As I listened to his story, I turned my Bible to Matthew 10:37–38, handed it to him, and said, "Read this out loud."

He read, "He that loveth father or mother more than me is not worthy of me: and he that loveth son or daughter more than me is not worthy of me. And he that taketh not his cross, and followeth after me, is not worthy of me."

I asked, "What does it say to you?"

He looked up at me and said, "I will worry about my mother later," and he bowed his head and accepted Christ as his personal Savior. He has been a deacon in his church for more than twelve years.

Are we guaranteed a happy ending when we share our faith with friends and family? According to Scripture, Jesus came to divide. He said, "Suppose ye that I am come to give peace on earth? I tell you, Nay; but rather division: For from henceforth there shall be five in one house divided, three against two, and two against three. The father shall be divided against the son, and the son against the father; the mother against the daughter, and the daughter against the mother; the mother in law against her daughter in law, and the daughter in law against her mother in law" (Luke 12:51–53).

When you surrender your life to Christ, it may cost you every relationship you have. You truly have to die to yourself, follow Christ, and leave your loved ones behind.

Murray became a believer. He decided to go share his faith with his parents, even though they had told him if he ever brought his religion into their house, he'd never be allowed to come back.

On his way to his parents' home, he stopped to see me, and we prayed together. After our prayer, he looked up with misty eyes and asked, "I don't have a choice, do I, Bill?"

I shook my head.

He said, "I can either stay in the sin of silence and say nothing, watching my parents stay condemned because they never heard the gospel, or I can choose to risk being permanently rejected by them forever."

I nodded.

He thought for a moment, then said, "The call's clear."

I said, "Yup."

So he went. He risked everything. He risked being separated from his family. Fortunately, Murray's story had a happy ending. He was overjoyed when both of his parents made a commitment to Christ. But things could have turned out very differently. And Murray was willing to take that chance, despite the personal cost.

6. I don't know how.

Sherry was determined to share her faith with her parents, George and Donna, so she wrote them a letter. Then she booked a plane for Texas for a visit. Later, when her parents took her to the airport to say good-bye, Sherry realized she had not shared her faith and broke into tears. Donna asked, "What's wrong, honey?"

Sherry said, "I came to tell you about the most important thing in my life, and we haven't talked about it."

Donna asked, "You mean the letter you wrote us?"

Sherry nodded.

Donna turned to Sherry's dad and said, "George, let this poor gal share."

But by that time, Sherry was so flustered that when she opened her Bible, she found it nothing but a blur of tears. When she tried to talk, she only rambled and sobbed.

Perhaps you were like Sherry, always wanting to share your faith but never knowing how.

Once you have studied the technique explained in this book (and follow the verses in the back of the Gideon PWT), you will find that sharing your faith is so simple, your only frustration will be that you will wish you'd known how to do it sooner.

Six months later, Sherry heard the presentation "Share Jesus without Fear." She was able to call her parents on the phone and use the approach to share the gospel with them.

Donna and George acknowledged they believed. Yet Sherry wasn't sure that their faith was rooted, because she found no evidence of it in their lives. But she said, "I was able to take my parents through the gospel, and I was able to at least get them to acknowledge the truth. This is a start."

Recently, two young women, Karen and Sharon, came up to me after a service and said, "Bill, would you pray for us? We're on our way to the hospital to see our father, who is dying of cancer. We've tried to share our faith with him before, but we've never gotten to first base. But what you've taught us tonight seems so simple, we want to try again."

A few days later, I got a call. Karen said, "Not only did we lead Dad to Christ, but his roommate overheard our conversation and asked, 'What about me?' He received Christ too! We are experiencing the joy of God in ways we have never known before because we realize we can no longer fail."

The PWT eliminates the excuse of not being confident enough to share the gospel message. The plan of salvation is clearly laid out on the last two pages of the back inside cover. Therefore, we have a basic framework to follow. Many have come to Christ, simply by reading these verses in sequence.

Drop Those Excuses

If you wish to experience the level of joy so many others have found, you will have to drop those excuses for not sharing your faith. You will have to practice obedience to the Great Commission. Not only will this impact the lives of your loved ones, giving the Holy Spirit the opportunity to draw them to Christ, but you will also experience a new depth in your relationship with God that you never experienced before. After all, God promised, "I will be with thee" (Exod. 3:12). Wait until you see what God will do with an ordinary person, like you, who is obedient in sharing his faith.

Chapter 4
THE SHARE JESUS QUESTIONS

I remember Dave Nicholl, a coach from Windsor, Colorado. Dave, like so many of us, had become complacent in sharing his faith. Days after his church began to pray that believers would develop a passion and brokenness for the lost, two teen boys from his high school were killed in a tragic incident at a party. The next day, God overhauled Dave's heart. He became convicted that the sin of silence would no longer be a part of his life.

Shortly thereafter, he had the opportunity to deliver gift books to the graduating seniors. As he visited the teens in their homes, he had many opportunities to present the gospel. Because of God's grace and Dave's commitment and follow-through, more than seventy people accepted Christ as their Savior in Windsor.

Dave said, "Although I've shared my faith in different ways through the years, the 'Share Jesus without Fear' approach has been the easiest to use. I simply present the questions and Scriptures to others. It's a process of give and take. The questions allow people to share their hearts, then the Scriptures allow the Holy Spirit to change their hearts. The results are incredible."

If Dave can do it, you can too. You just need to know the right questions to ask.

Conversation Joggers

We talked about how it takes an average of 7.6 times for someone to hear the gospel before he receives it. How do we know whose heart has arrived at that 7.6 average? We don't know unless we ask probing questions to find out where God is at work so we can join him.

Asking probing questions is a lot like using a meat thermometer. Think about cooking at home. Whenever you cook a roast, you will usually use a meat thermometer to see what is going on inside the meat. Otherwise, with variables like the thickness of the roast or changes in the oven temperature, how will you know when it's done?

Now I can't walk around with a thermometer in my hand, asking people, "Are you cooking?" But I can insert a question into conversation to try to determine if God is at work and to see if their hearts are open. For example, if I am speaking with a woman, I may ask her, "What do you think is the biggest problem women face today?" Sometimes I tease her and add, "And your answer cannot be 'men!'"

She may chuckle to herself before pointing to the problem of time pressure.

I say, "One minute you are told to be supermom, the next minute, super-career-woman. I don't have a clue how a woman does it in today's society. By the way, do you have any spiritual beliefs?"

Did you see the switch? In the middle of any conversation, I can insert any one of the five "Share Jesus Questions," which we are about to review, to see if God is at work. Do you see how simple it is to insert a spiritual thermometer?

By using the final question, "Do you have any spiritual beliefs?" we are suddenly on the track I want to take. We are running toward the gospel of Jesus Christ.

Sometimes I might ask a man, "What's your favorite sport?"

Often his response is, "Football."

I'll say, "It's amazing how much money some athletes make. Then you realize their lives are trashed on drugs and domestic abuse. Have you ever wondered how much money it takes for a man's life to be perfect?"

He often says, "It takes a lot."

I reply, "Yes, it does. Do you have any spiritual beliefs?"

Suddenly, we have moved from talking about sports to spirituality in only one question.

Another favorite conversation jogger I use is, "By the way, do you go to church anywhere?"

I often get answers like, "My cousin is a pastor in Nebraska," or "I go to the big white one, but I can't think of the name of it." Answers like this always send up a red flag.

Once I asked this question in a restaurant in Alaska. As the waitress refilled my glass of tea, I asked, "Do you go to church anywhere?"

She turned deep red. I thought she was going to faint, but she took a couple of steps back and said, "I've been thinking about that for the last couple of weeks."

Bingo! We were off on a spiritual conversation.

Once I was sitting next to a woman on an airplane. At the end of the flight, I asked, "Is this the end of your trip?"

"Yes."

"Who do you work for?"

"I'm an engineer for Hughes Aircraft."

"That's wonderful. Do you go to church anywhere?"

She responded, "I'm Coptic Catholic."

We had about two and a half minutes before the plane pulled to the gate.

Then I asked a question I've never asked before, "How does a Coptic Catholic get saved?"

She looked at me and said, "I've been wondering about that."

Oh boy, here was a 7.6, and we were out of time. Suddenly the captain came on with an announcement. I froze because I wanted to tell her how to get saved; she froze because she wanted to hear what I had to say. When I heard the captain's announcement, I chuckled because I forgot my own teaching. God is sovereign and in control. The captain said, "I'm sorry, ladies and gentlemen, we cannot go to the gate right now. There is a plane at the gate, so we have to go to the penalty box."

She laughed, and I had to smile. *Lord, you are sovereign.*

We had more than enough time. I was able to share and watch her invite Christ into her heart.

Another great way to lead the conversation to Christ is simply to ask, "Have you ever received a free copy of God's Word?" If there is any interest, take out your PWT and start to show them the "Helps" section in the front. As previously stated, they often warm up to you when they see the Bible was written to help them. Perhaps this will open the conversation for one of the five "Share Jesus Questions."

These conversation joggers will help ease you into a God-pointing conversation of your own. And if you need another idea, try this simple experiment. Go to a neighbor, a friend, or relative and say, "I wonder if you could help me with a five-question survey?"

The next thing you know, you are on your way to sharing your faith.

The Five Questions

I remember sitting with John in a restaurant. I had been introduced by a friend who had brought him. We chatted a little before I turned to John and asked, "Do you have any kind of spiritual belief?"

"Yes," John answered, "I've been involved with several religions. I've attended a Catholic church, tried Christian Science, and have studied world religions."

My response was, "Hmmmmm."

I asked, "What's your understanding of who Jesus Christ is?"

"He was a man who was probably a good man and a teacher and prophet who tried to make a difference on this earth."

"Hmmmmm," I said. "Do you think there is a heaven or hell?"

"I don't know," John replied. "Sometimes earth feels like hell."

I smiled and asked, "If you were to die, where would you go?"

John said, "If there is an up, I hope I'd go there."

"Why would God let you into heaven?"

"I've led a basically moral life," John replied.

Then with my best smile, I said, "If what you were believing is not true, would you want to know?"

"Absolutely," John said.

Notice what happened. At the end of my questioning, John gave me *permission* to share my faith with him. I did, and I'm happy to report that John accepted Christ as his Savior and has walked with Jesus for more than eight years.

Why do you think John and I did not fight? Why did we not get into disagreements of intellect and world religions? How did we avoid an argument?

It is because I asked him a question.

Why are questions effective? For one thing, most folks have opinions on almost every subject, and they love to share them. Second, questions work because they put you, the questioner, in control without putting your friend on the defensive.

You keep the questioning friendly because you never try to force someone to agree with you. Instead, all you need to do is to sit back and listen to his answers.

The Hmmmmm Principle

When I'm asking these questions, no matter what the responder says, I never answer. All you get from me is "Hmmmmm." As many husbands and wives know, it is difficult to have an argument with someone who is just "hmmmmming."

Even so, there is a principle at work here. This principle reminds us that if you really care—really love someone—you will listen, attentively. As you listen to what your friend is saying, through the power of the Holy Spirit, you may be able to hear if your friend is dealing with problems like loneliness, emptiness, pain, or anger. You will be able to discern how close his heart is to God.

The five "Share Jesus Questions" you can ask, are:

1. Do you have any kind of spiritual beliefs?

2. To you, who is Jesus Christ?
3. Do you think there is a heaven or hell?
4. If you died, where would you go? If heaven, why?
5. If what you are believing is not true, would you want to know?

These questions act as a funnel. You can start these questions anywhere on the list, as you feel led. The first question I generally ask acts as an ice-breaker. It is:

1. Do you have any kind of spiritual beliefs?

I never ask, "Do you believe in God?" because that question is often considered offensive. The person to whom I'm speaking may feel his or her belief in God is none of my business. Even so, most people are happy to reply to a question about spiritual beliefs because they love to give their opinions.

When I ask the spiritual-belief question, some people will give me a two-second answer, and some people will give a ten-minute answer. The length of their response does not matter. What matters is you are listening as they open their spiritual hearts to you.

I can remember standing in line at a local restaurant. The woman in front of me was decked out in New Age, occult jewelry. I couldn't resist asking her, "Why do you wear all that?"

She told me she was a shaman, a white witch. "Do you have time for some coffee?" I asked.

"Sure."

I sat down at the community coffee table and asked her, "Do you have any kind of spiritual belief?"

My watch ticked off twenty-two minutes as she explained her faith in witchcraft, and all I said was, "Hmmmmm."

As a type A personality, I could barely sit still because I wanted to jump in and try to fix her. Instead, I listened in love.

Whether it's the witch who talks for twenty-two minutes or someone who quickly responds, "Yes, I have a spiritual belief," I don't give a response. I just ask the next question.

2. To you, who is Jesus Christ?

This question separates religious people from relational people. Religious people will often answer by saying something like, "Jesus is the son of God or a man who died on the cross. He's God's only begotten Son."

This is a correct theological statement, but it is very impersonal.

If I were to ask you this very same question, I hope you would answer, "He is *my* Lord and *my* Savior."

Did you hear the "my" in your voice? Your answer demonstrates you have a personal relationship with Christ.

3. Do you believe in heaven or hell?

A lady dropped by my house to try to sell me something. When she came in, the first question I asked her was, "Do you believe in heaven or hell?"

"Absolutely not," she responded.

Then I asked the next question.

4. If you died, where would you go?

The woman answered, "Heaven, of course."

Isn't it interesting that this woman believed she would go to a place she just said she didn't believe in? That's because she went from "head" belief to "heart" belief.

You may follow up with another question: "Why would God let you in?"

That brings us to the last question to help you get where you want to go. This is the question that will give you permission to open your Bible and share Scripture.

5. If what you are believing is not true, would you want to know?

This is a crucial question. People fear missing opportunities because of not knowing the right information.

There are only two possible answers to this question: yes or no. If the answer is yes, you have permission to go on to the next phase.

I'll give you a very surprising statement. Not once in the past sixteen years of asking this question have I ever had a no that stuck.

Let me clarify. If I said to someone, "If what you are believing is not true, would you want to know?" I might receive an emphatic, "No!"

I am silent.

The next thing I hear is, "Bill, aren't you going to tell me?"

I answer, "I thought you didn't want to know."

Most often the person says, "Yes, I do."

And here we go again. I then open my Bible and allow that person to read selected Scriptures, which we will discuss in the next chapter.

Use as Needed

You should note, that you can bypass conversational joggers and head straight for any one of the five "Share Jesus Questions" to use in any order. For instance, not long ago, by tossing out a "Share Question," I discovered a person who was already at that 7.6.

I was at the airport and I walked up to an airline employee. I said, "I love asking Continental people a question."

She glared over the top of her bifocals, "What do you want to know?"

"I'm curious," I said. "If you died right now, where would you go?"

Her face softened. "That's the most important question anyone has ever asked me."

It was so simple to find out God was working in her life. It was a privilege to join him and to go on to share my faith with her. I sat down with her and presented the gospel. It was a thrill to see her open her heart to Christ.

You Can't Fail

As you begin to ask these five questions, I think you will be amazed at how open people are. But please remember your motive for evangelism must be your love for God and love for people. This is not a thing you are doing; it is an act of consecration and belief in Jesus Christ. Pray daily for God to put opportunities in your path. Just as Jesus worked wherever his Father worked, so must you.

"Then answered Jesus and said unto them, 'Verily, verily, I say unto you, The Son can do nothing of himself, but what he seeth the Father do: for what things soever he doeth, these also doeth the Son likewise'" (John 5:19).

As you look around this week, ask, "Father, where are you working? Where can I join you?"

Pull out your spiritual thermometer and slip a "Share Question" into a conversation with a friend. If you discern God is at work, join him by showing your friend the "Share Jesus Scriptures." But regardless of your friend's response, never be discouraged if you don't have a conversation that leads to the sinner's prayer. For you cannot fail. Remember, success is sharing your faith and living your life out for Jesus Christ. It has nothing whatsoever to do with bringing anyone to the Lord.

Overcome Fear

You may be saying in your mind and heart, "I'm afraid to share my faith."

That is perfectly OK. The apostle Paul went to share his faith with much fear, weakness, and trembling. But still he went. I can't make you a promise your fear will go away completely, but it will get easier. I promise you your faith in God will go to an entirely new level as you share your faith.

I can remember when I surprised Wendy, a wonderful Christian neighbor who was very shy. She was always pushing her baby around our neighborhood in a stroller. One day, she was pushing her baby by my house, and I said, "I understand you are a Christian."

"Uh-huh."

"Where do you go to church?" I asked.

When she told me, I turned and called up to Paul, who was fixing rain gutters on my roof.

"Paul, there is someone I want you to meet." Paul came down the ladder and stood politely.

I said, "Paul, Wendy is going to share her faith and tell you how to meet Jesus Christ."

And I walked off.

Wendy's eyes were as big as saucers. But even under the pressure, she trusted God and shared her faith, and Paul came to the Lord.

God is sovereign, and hell will not prevail against you. There is no possible way you can mess this up. What God wants to teach you is that he can work through your life despite your personality, lack of spiritual gifts, or talents. Because you see, Coach Dave Nicholl is not the only one God wants to use. There is no insignificant Christian, for we all have the power of the Holy Spirit dwelling within us. I hope this week, as well as the rest of your life, you are going to walk around in anticipation of what God is about to do in your life. You will be in constant prayer, "God, are you at work over here, over there?"

And like the seemingly insignificant shoe salesman who led the future evangelist D. L. Moody to Christ, won't it be exciting as God uses you to give him glory?

Catch the Excitement

I got a call from an officer in law enforcement about an awards banquet at which I was to pray the benediction the next evening. I said to Will, "Let's have lunch today."

He said, "I can't. I've got to go over and see Jeannie. Do you remember her? She's getting an award tomorrow."

"Is she the woman who was paralyzed when she tried to protect a man at a bus stop and got shot herself?"

"You bet she is," Will said.

I said, "But, Will, her award is only temporary. What are you going to do about giving her an award that will last forever?"

Will's response was immediate. "Meet me at the Conoco."

I met Will, and he took me over to Jeannie's one-bedroom apartment.

God is in control. Her brother and physical therapist just happened to be leaving. We had her all to ourselves. I looked into Jeannie's smiling face and said, "My name is Chaplain Bill Fay, and I came by to ask you a few questions. Do you go to church anywhere?"

"Yes, I am Baptist, but I am not saved."

"How come?"

"I smoke cigarettes."

I took her through the questions and Scriptures, then I held her hand as she prayed to receive Christ.

I could hear Will walking around her apartment. His hands were straight up in the air, his finger pointing to God. He exclaimed, "God is good all the time! All the time God is good!"

The next day, at the awards banquet, Jeannie said, "I accept this award on behalf of Jesus Christ who first saved my life and then gave me eternal life."

I looked over, and Will stood up in the back and started walking around again, saying, "God is good all the time! All the time God is good!"

If you want to start experiencing the joy and excitement that Will found, start sharing your faith.

Review

Optional Conversation Joggers
Review the complete list in appendix 1.

The Five Share Jesus Questions

These questions act as a funnel. You can start anywhere on the list, as you feel led, or you can skip to the "Share Jesus Scriptures."

1. Do you have any kind of spiritual belief?
2. To you, who is Jesus?
3. Do you think there is a heaven or a hell?
4. If you died, where would you go? If heaven, why?
5. If what you are believing is not true, would you want to know?

You might ask at this point, "May I share some Scriptures with you?" If the answer is yes, open your Bible to the next phase. If the answer is no, do nothing. But remember you have not failed. You have been obedient to share the gospel, and the results belong to God.

Note: This, as well as other phases of the "Share Presentation," can be found in abbreviated form in appendix 1 for quick reference.

Chapter 5
THE POWER OF SCRIPTURE

So far you've learned you cannot fail when you are obedient to share your faith. You've also learned how to ask questions as conversation starters. The answers to these questions will help you determine if God is at work in the life of the person with whom you are sharing. Plus, when you ask, "By the way, if what you were believing is not true, would you want to know it?" you will most likely win permission to go to the next step: to share the power of God's Word.

The Power of God's Word

God's Word penetrates and changes hearts toward his Son. Hebrews 4:12 says, "For the word of God is quick, and powerful, and sharper than any twoedged sword, piercing even to the dividing asunder of soul and spirit, and of the joints and marrow, and is a discerner of the thoughts and intents of the heart."

Do you remember what you were like before you became a believer? The Bible probably had little or no meaning to you or your life. Yet somehow, when you became a Christian, the Bible seemed different.

The Bible didn't change; you changed. You became a new creation. Suddenly, this book became alive with meaning about life and eternity.

The Bible says a man without the Spirit does not understand the things of the spirit (1 Cor. 2:14).

So, how in the world can you reach someone who cannot understand God's love? *You* cannot. That is the job of the Holy Spirit. The Holy Spirit will move through God's Word.

The Scripture Principles

There are two basic principles at work when you share Scripture. The first comes from Romans 10:17: "So then faith cometh by hearing, and hearing by the word of God."

The second principle comes from Luke 10:26, which describes Jesus' approach to a man who was reading the Law. Jesus simply asked the man, "How readest thou?" In other words, Jesus was asking, "What does this say to you?"

In this way, Jesus was able to discuss Scripture without starting an argument. What a great example—an example you can follow when sharing Scripture from the Bible!

"What does this say to you?" is a question. It is not a defense or an argument. All you have to do is listen to your friend's answer. Your only job is to turn pages and to stay out of God's way. The Holy Spirit will help your friend understand more from a simple reading of a verse than any explanation or sermon you could have preached.

Big Boomer versus the Derringer

But before you pull out the big Bible you use in your quiet time, the one I refer to as "Big Boomer," let me hold up a red flag. Before I was a believer, I had a hard time being with Christians, let alone being with their Big Boomers. Perhaps, instead of pulling out what looks like a cannon in the eyes of a nonbeliever, you could pull out a little derringer, the kind you can hide in your pocket until you need it.

The Gideon Personal Worker's Testament (PWT) is ideal for this purpose. It is small enough to slip into your pocket or purse.

Your Commitment

This PWT represents your commitment. When you carry it, you are saying you are living under the anticipation that God is going to move in your life.

Have you ever left your wallet on the dresser or left your purse in your car? You run around feeling empty and lost. That's the way it should be when you leave your PWT behind. It should become such a part of you that you feel lost without it.

Objections to the Bible

You may get one of two objections when you open your PWT. Your friend may say the Bible has:

- Too many errors.

This objection is answered in this simple script:

Friend: There are many errors in the Bible.

You: *(Don't go off on a rabbit trail. Instead, with all the love you can muster, hand your friend your PWT.)* Would you show me one?

Friend: Well, I can't.

You: I can't either. Let's turn to Romans 3:23.

- Too many translations.

When someone says to me, "There are many translations of the Bible," I give him my Denver Seminary answer—an answer that cost me about fifteen grand to obtain. So don't miss it! I answer this statement by simply saying, "Yep."

You see, the nonbeliever thinks he's "gotcha." And when you say to him, "Did you know you are absolutely right? There are many translations of Scriptures. But did you know they all say the same thing?"

The nonbeliever says, "No, I didn't!" and you say, "Let's turn to Romans 3:23."

Let's examine Scripture for a moment. For two thousand years, men and women have studied this book to prove it true or false. Isn't it interesting no one ever found an error? Think about it this way, if your heavenly Father can't write a book without a proven error, why would you expect him to be able to get you out of a grave?

In fact, I would concede that if anyone found a genuine error in the manuscripts, my faith would have been in vain. No matter how you examine it, historically, prophetically, or archaeologically, it remains flawless. God promised that not one crossed *t* or dotted *i* came about by the will of man. Man did not write or create the Bible. Instead, man was inspired and carried along by the power of the Holy Spirit to write down God's inerrant Word. (Please note that these and other objections and their responses can be found in chap. 8 as well as app. 2.)

Share Scriptures

The second step in sharing Jesus without fear is to allow the Bible to speak. God uses Scripture to change people's lives. You will provide a series of Bible verses to ask your friend to read out loud. These verses are found on the last two pages of the PWT:

1. John 3:16
2. Romans 5:8
3. Romans 3:23
4. Romans 3:10
5. Romans 6:23
6. John 1:12
7. 1 Corinthians 15:3–4

8. Revelation 3:20a
9. Romans 10:13

You will note in the PWT that these verses are categorized into four different parts of the plan of salvation. It is important that they read *at least* one verse in each section.

How to Use the Share Scriptures

This step couldn't be easier. Turn your PWT (open to the back inside cover) toward your friend and say:

You: Read this aloud.

Friend: *(Reads Scripture out loud.)*

You: What does this say to you?

Friend: *(Answers correctly.)*

You: *(Point to the next Scripture.)* Read this aloud.

He cannot say, "That's your interpretation" because he's done all the reading and analyzing. The Holy Spirit, not you, is in charge of all the convincing and convictions. You are simply pointing out the Scriptures with one goal: to stay out of God's way.

Read It Out Loud

Why did I have my friend read it out loud? Because faith comes from hearing.

When people read Scripture aloud, you will be surprised how quickly they become convinced of their need to trust Jesus as Lord and Savior. Watch God at work as you continue to guide others to read these Scriptures.

Share Scripture Script

To show you how to use this technique, I have provided a script for each Scripture. Don't let this script intimidate you. It is only meant to show you how easy it is to ask your friend:

1. "Read this Scripture aloud," *and*
2. "What does this say to you?"

This script is that simple. It does not contain a lot of other material to memorize.

When you get a positive response to the question "By the way, if what you were believing is not true, would you want to know?" it is time to pull out your PWT. Turn the PWT to the last two pages and point to John 3:16.

- **Verse One: John 3:16—"God loves you."**

You: *(Point to the verse in your PWT.)* Read this aloud.

Friend: *(Reading:)* For God so loved the world, that he gave his only begotten Son, that whosoever believeth in him should not perish, but have everlasting life.

You: What does this say to you?

Friend: (*You are looking for an answer like:)* God loves me.

Point to Romans 3:23.

- **Verse Two: Romans 3:23—"All are sinners."**

You: *(Point to Romans 3:23 in your PWT.)* Read this aloud.

Friend: *(Reading:)* For all have sinned, and come short of the glory of God.

You: What does this say to you?

Friend: (*You are looking for an answer like:)* Everyone has sinned.

Note: You don't have to take time to explain sin, although you may want to point out the divine standard for humanity is perfection. Most of us readily admit we don't know anyone who is perfect as God is perfect. The Bible tells us that "there is none that doeth good, no, not one" (Rom. 3:12). This means all people have sinned and do not reflect God's righteousness and perfection. Also, see response 16 in chapter 8 or appendix 2 if your friend does not believe he is a sinner.

- **Verse Three: Romans 6:23—"For the wages of sin is death."**

Note: The reason Romans 6:23 is important is because many lost people hope their actions, such as baptism or membership in a church, will get them to heaven. This Scripture allows the Holy Spirit to show there is no hope of heaven without faith in Jesus and surrendering to live for him.

You: Read this aloud.

Friend: *(Reading:)* For the wages of sin is death; but the gift of God is eternal life through Jesus Christ our Lord.

You: What does this say to you?

Friend: (*You are looking for an answer like:)* The result of sin is death, but God gives life through his Son.

You: *(Point to the word* sin.*)* Did you notice the word *sin*?

Friend: Yes.

You: *(Point to yourself so you don't come across as holding yourself above being a sinner.)* This reminds us there is no *s* at the end of the word. God says one sin will send me to hell.

You: Did you notice the word *death?* In the Bible, death often refers to hell.

You: *(Point to the word* through.) This word reminds us that becoming a Christian means you have to be in a *relationship* with Jesus Christ, not in a religion.

I was asked to talk to a young woman who was in jail for murder. After asking her the five "Share Jesus Questions," I determined no one had ever shared about Jesus or Christianity with her. When I asked her what Romans 6:23 meant, she said, "I need to ask God to forgive me for all my sins and invite Jesus Christ into my heart." I was surprised. Does that verse say that? Not exactly. Where did she get her answer? The Holy Spirit.

I did not say, "Hold it. I have three more verses." We stopped, and she invited Christ into her life to forgive her of her sins right then and there.

We must be open. Through the power of Scripture, God may reveal truth in one verse or several verses. Simply point to the verses and ask questions.

- **Verse Four: 1 Corinthians 15:3–4—"Christ died and rose for our sins."**

You: *(Point to 1 Corinthians 15:3–4.)* Read this aloud.

Friend: *(Reading:)* For I delivered unto you first of all that which I also received, how that Christ died for our sins according to the scriptures; And that he was buried, and that he rose again the third day according to the scriptures:

You: What does this verse say to you?

Friend: *(You are looking for an answer like:)* That Jesus Christ died and rose from the dead for our sins.

- **Verse Five: John 1:12—"God's remedy for sin."**

You: *(Point to John 1:12.)* Read this aloud.

Friend: *(Reading:)* But as many as received him, to them gave he power to become the sons of God, even to them that believe on his name:

You: What does this verse say to you?

Friend: *(You are looking for an answer like:)* We need to receive Jesus Christ.

I would like to point out as you are sharing Scripture, you do not have to explain or discredit false teachings. The key to sharing Jesus without fear is to present what the Bible says and let it stand on its own.

Note: One of the most difficult things for many people to believe is that they can be forgiven. You may not have knowledge of the lost person's sins, but you can be sure most lost people have particular sins they'll be thinking about and considering. The person may be thinking about adultery, alcoholism, hatred toward a spouse or an enemy, a bitter heart, living with a lie about a past experience, or any of a multitude of sins that burden people. You do your part by showing your friend the Word of God. It is through the Word that God will pour his power. If for some reason your friend doesn't understand or misunderstands the Scripture, please don't correct him. Just say, "Read it again!"

Remember you couldn't "fix" yourself, so don't expect to fix others. Please stay out of the way and let the Holy Spirit do his job.

- **Verse Six: Revelation 3:20a—"All May Be Saved."**

You: *(Point to Revelation 3:20a.)* Read this aloud.

Friend: *(Reading:)* "Behold, I stand at the door, and knock: if any man hear my voice, and open the door, I will come in to him."

You: What does this say to you?

Friend: (*You are looking for an answer like:)* If I ask Jesus to come into my life, he will.

Note: You want your friend to understand that opening his heart to Jesus is his choice. Jesus is eager to come into our lives, but he never forces open the door.

That's it! You've just finished sharing the Scriptures. Check appendix 1 or the review at the end of this chapter for quick reference.

Note: If your friend gives the wrong answer, have her read it again out loud until she understands it on her own accord. The lost person must understand that salvation—promised through Jesus' death—comes to all who surrender their lives to him in faith. We all are on level ground at the cross. When we surrender to Christ as Savior, we are inwardly transformed to have new life. When we surrender our lives to Christ in faith, we no longer are slaves to sin and selfish desires. We have hearts turned to Jesus and his example for how we should live. The Christian heart is freed by the power of the Holy Spirit from being self-centered to being Christ-centered. A Christ-centered heart will be filled with love for others.

Read It Again

What happens when someone doesn't understand the Scripture? You simply say, "Read it again."

Now let's see if I can trick you. I would like to pretend you are sharing the last Scripture, Revelation 3:20, with me. You've got your Bible facing me, and you have just asked me to read the Scripture.

Bill: *(Reading:)* "Behold, I stand at the door, and knock: if any man hear my voice, and open the door, I will come in to him."

You: What does it say to you?

Bill: If Jesus is opening the door, Jesus is coming in.

I hope you caught it. I gave you the wrong answer. Jesus never crashes a party. He does not go where he is not invited. If you caught that, good for you. If not, think how tender it is to say, "Read it again."

One time I got a phone call at two in the morning from a pastor who did not want to deal with an intoxicated seventeen-year-old boy. I remember when Todd called me. He was so drunk he vomited on the telephone and fell off his bed screaming. Yet he agreed to meet me the next day. I figured only the Holy Spirit could help him to remember our conversation. I borrowed Frank Armenta, a friend of mine. Frank was on heroin for twenty-eight years before he found Jesus Christ. I didn't borrow Frank because of his inner-city experience; I borrowed Frank because he was the biggest guy I could think of! When I got to the restaurant, I realized I didn't have a clue what Todd looked like. I figured out if he really was that drunk last night, I would be able to spot him. Sure enough, here came a guy who looked like death warmed over. I looked at him and asked, "Are you Todd?"

When he said yes, I could see tears in his eyes.

I turned to him and Frank and said, "Let's get out of here."

It was a hot day, and we got in my car and rolled down the windows. We drove down the road to find a place that was cool. We stopped in front of a shady tree that happened to be in front of the Denver County Jail.

Frank sat and prayed while I asked Todd to read Romans 10:9–11 out loud.

He read, "That if thou shalt confess with thy mouth the Lord Jesus, and shalt believe in thine heart that God hath raised him from the dead, thou shalt be saved. For with the heart man believeth unto righteousness; and with the mouth confession is made unto salvation. For the scripture saith, Whosoever believeth on him shall not be ashamed."

I asked, "What does this say to you?"

Suddenly, another voice—a demonic voice—came out of Todd and said, "It cannot save him."

My hair stood straight up. I ignored the voice and said, "Read it again." After all, I'm not going to fight with this demon. Let God defend his Word; he's been doing it for eternity.

Todd read it again out loud, and the voice got nastier. "It cannot save him or anyone else."

We repeated this process, ten to twelve times before the Word of God broke through. As it did, a horrible shriek rose from Todd as the nasty spirit left.

Todd was weeping in the back of my car, broken for his sin. Suddenly, his hands shot up as he praised God. For ten minutes he alternated between weeping and praising God. Did you ever have a silly thought that comes in from nowhere? After about ten minutes of watching Todd, weeping over his sins and praising God, I remember, this silly thought came into my head: *What in the world am I going to do if a cop comes along?*

Because I hated to be alone in my stupidity, I jolted Frank from his prayer by tapping his leg and asked, "Have you ever seen anything like this?"

"Yeah," he said. "At my own conversion."

We both laughed and praised God. The good news is, ten years later Todd is still active in the church and free from the power of darkness, all because of the Word of God.

Another time, I remember sitting with a young lady named Sharon. I turned to Romans 3:23 and said, "Would you read this out loud?" She did. I said, "What does it say to you?"

She said, "I don't believe what it says."

I said, "Read it again."

She did. I asked, "What does it say?"

She said, "I don't believe there's sin."

"Read it again," I said. She read it again.

I asked, "What does it say?"

She said, "I don't believe in sin."

I said, "Read it again."

She did.

"What does it say?" I asked.

"Well," she said, "it says we have all sinned, doesn't it?"

I smiled because God's Word had done the work, and I said, "Yes. Does that include you?"

She said, "Yes."

She continued on in the Scriptures, then gave her life to Jesus Christ. I will never forget the sight of her weeping over the fact she was forgiven. God is good!

Review

The following is a quick review of the Scriptures you will share with your friends and family. Remember, ask them to read the verses aloud, then ask, "What does this say to you?"

1. John 3:16—"God loves you."

"For God so loved the world, that he gave his only begotten Son, that whosoever believeth in him should not perish, but have everlasting life."

What does this say to you?

2. Romans 3:23—"All are sinners."

"For all have sinned, and come short of the glory of God."

What does this say to you?

3. Romans 6:23—"For the wages of sin is death."

"For the wages of sin is death; but the gift of God is eternal life through Jesus Christ our Lord."

What does this say to you?

4. 1 Corinthians 15:3–4—"Christ died and rose for our sins."

"For I delivered unto you first of all that which I also received, how that Christ died for our sins according to the scriptures; And that he was buried, and that he rose again the third day according to the scriptures."

What does this say to you?

5. John 1:12—"God's remedy for sin."

"But as many as received him, to them gave he power to become the sons of God, even to them that believe on his name."

What does this say to you?

6. Revelation 3:20a—"All may be saved now."

"Behold, I stand at the door, and knock: if any man hear my voice, and open the door, I will come in to him."

What does this say to you?

Decision Time

Now you have seen the power of God work through his Scripture. It is time to help your friend come to a decision about what he will do about God.

Chapter 6
BRING TO DECISION

After I finished teaching a seminar one night, a gentleman came over to thank me for the evening.

I asked him, "Do you know Christ yet?"

Glen said, "I'm still trying to find him."

"Tell me about yourself," I said.

"I'm an engineer, and my marriage is on the rocks." He sighed. "I have a lot of questions about faith."

I said, "Let's do a spiritual check and see where you are stuck. Are you a sinner?"

"Yes."

"Do you want forgiveness of your sins?"

"Yes."

"Do you believe Jesus died on the cross and rose again?"

He shook his head. "I don't know."

"Glen, if you could be sure that Jesus died and rose again, would you want your sins forgiven?"

He nodded solemnly.

"Let's talk about the Resurrection. God made sure that in history there was evidence to the reality of Jesus Christ. Glen, would you be willing to ask God to help you in your unbelief?"

"Yes, I am willing."

I put my hand on his shoulder. "God is about to listen to your heart. Let's try a simple prayer and see God move."

We bowed our heads, and Glen repeated after me, "I am a sinner. I want forgiveness of all my sins. I want to believe that Jesus died on the cross for my sin. Help me in my unbelief. Father, if this is true, help me in my marriage. I want to give Jesus my life."

Glen looked up from his prayer. His eyes glistened with joy. "It's all true," he confessed for the first time. "I believe!"

I asked, "Glen, where's Jesus?"

He grinned. "In my heart."

"Is your wife here?"

"Yes, I'll go get her."

When Renee came, we found out she had just given her heart to Christ in the prayer room. Then we found their twelve-year-old daughter, Theresa, who was all teary-eyed.

"What's going on?" I asked.

Theresa started to cry. "I don't know if I should live with my dad in Oklahoma or my mom and stepdad here."

I asked, "Theresa, can you see tomorrow?"

"No," she whispered.

"I know one who can. Who do you think that is?"

She looked up. "Jesus?"

"Have you ever known Jesus?"

"No, but I heard the gospel tonight. How do you receive Jesus?"

I joyfully took her over to her mom and dad, who were talking to the pastor, and said, "Your daughter is ready to join you in a relationship with Jesus Christ." Soon after, Theresa prayed to receive Jesus as her Lord.

When you are in the business of sharing your faith, it's not just one life that will be made whole; it may be a family, village, state, or nation. The question is, do you want the privilege?

This family followed me out of the church, thanking me. But I am the one who is thankful to God. It is such a privilege to be used by him in this way.

The Choice

Obviously, we look for the opportunity to present the gospel to people. Yet we would be remiss if we did not give people a choice, the choice to receive life or death. My cowriter, Linda, found this concept to be true on a busy beach in Galveston, Texas, when she was a teen. She says,

> I was sixteen years old and was at the sea wall with my youth group to share our faith. I was nervous, but my anxiety was soon lulled by the waves rolling onto the beach below and by the blue sky stretching above. As I handed out printed gospel tracts, I walked by a seashell shop. My partner, Stephanie, and I discovered two hiding coworkers. "What's the matter?" I asked them.
>
> Carol held back tears. "We were handing out tracts when we ran into a man who asked a question we couldn't answer."
>
> "What did he ask?" I demanded.
>
> "He wanted to know if God was so great, could he make a wall so strong, even he couldn't break it? Then he wanted to know if God was so great, why couldn't he break the wall?"
>
> "Oh!" I responded, deflating like a punctured balloon. I turned to face a salty breeze, wondering if the question was a trick or if my faith was flawed.
>
> A Scripture from Psalm 69:32 drifted into my thoughts: "And your heart shall live that seek God."
>
> "I know the answer!" I exclaimed. "God has already created a wall like that. It's the human heart." Although God's mighty enough, he'll never break through the wall. He will enter only if invited in.

God is a gentleman; he never forces us to love or to serve him. Joshua made this same discovery. About fourteen hundred years before the birth of Christ, he was called to lead the tribes of Israel across the Jordan River into the land God was about to give them. Later, as he assembled all the tribes before God, he reminded the people how God had brought their forefathers from Egypt and had delivered them from warring nations. Joshua told them, "Now therefore fear the LORD, and serve him in sincerity and in truth: . . . And if it seem evil unto you to serve the LORD, choose you this day whom ye will serve; . . . but as for me and my house, we will serve the LORD" (Josh. 24:14–15).

Just as in the days of Joshua, God still offers his love and the opportunity to serve him, but he will not force it on anyone. You may recall God once before offered the tribes of Israel the land across the Jordan. They refused this blessing out of fear of the people who lived there. Because they refused this blessing, they were left to wander in the desert for forty years until Joshua finally led them to victory. It is clear. It is our choice to receive God's blessing and to serve him, or not.

When we look at Jesus' ministry on earth, we see he always gave people a choice. For example, Jesus asked the invalid at the pool of Bethesda if he wanted to be healed. Imagine, this man had been crippled for thirty-eight years. He sat on his mat by the pool at the Sheep Gate, surrounded by the sick and lame. Each hoped to be first in the pool if the Lord sent an angel to stir the waters with healing. Yet Jesus made no assumptions.

He asked the lame man, "Wilt thou be made whole?

"The impotent man answered him, Sir, I have no man, when the water is troubled, to put me into the pool: but while I am coming, another steppeth down before me.

"Jesus saith unto him, Rise, take up thy bed, and walk. And immediately the man was made whole, and took up his bed, and walked: and on the same day was the sabbath" (John 5:6–9).

Isn't it interesting that Jesus didn't force the crippled man to receive restoration? As a matter of fact, Jesus never forced his healing or love on anyone. So it takes more than hearing the gospel to become born again. It comes down to making a choice about what you have heard.

Wouldn't it be awful if you showed someone God's love but did not give him the choice to receive it? That's what D. L. Moody once did, and it haunted him the rest of his life.

"He did not ask an audience to receive Christ as Savior on April 8, 1871, the night of the Chicago fire. That night Moody spoke to his largest audience ever in Chicago. His topic was 'What Then Shall I Do with Jesus Who Is Called the Christ?' At the conclusion, he asked the listeners to consider the question and respond the next Sunday, when they returned. But they did not return. Fire bells rang even as they rose, and the building burned, and the congregation scattered."[1]

Moody always wondered how many of his audience came to faith before they slipped into eternity.

We need to offer others a choice. You will be surprised how easy it will be to share your faith, to say, "By the way, if what you are believing is not true, would you want to know it?" When you receive a yes to this question, you can move on to direct your friend to read Scripture aloud and ask, "What does it say to you?"

Let's pretend your friend has read the six "Share Jesus Scriptures" and has now responded to the last verse, Revelation 3:20a: "Behold, I stand at the door, and knock: if any man hear my voice, and open the door, I will come in to him." When this last Scripture has been read aloud, it's time to ask five more questions. The following "Commitment Questions" are also found on the pocket card attached to the back cover of this book:

1. Are you a sinner?
2. Do you want forgiveness of sins?
3. Do you believe Jesus died on the cross for you and rose again?
4. Are you willing to surrender your life to Jesus Christ?
5. Are you ready to invite Jesus into your life and into your heart?

The following is a discussion of these questions:

1. Are you a sinner?

This first question is based on the first read-aloud Scripture, Romans 3:23: "All have sinned." The "Share Jesus Scriptures" prepare the listeners' hearts for the "Commitment Questions" you are now asking.

Next ask:

2. Do you want forgiveness of sins?

We've already pointed out, in Romans 6:23, the wages of sin is death. So by now your friend should know why he needs forgiveness. It is his *choice*. It is up to him to receive it or not.

3. Do you believe Jesus died on the cross for you and rose again?

This is a key element in anyone's decision because the cross is central to the gospel. For as your friend read in 1 Corinthians 15:3–4, Christ died, was buried, and rose again the third day for our sins.

4. Are you willing to surrender your life to Jesus Christ?

This is a very important question. I'm always concerned about the possibility I might lead someone to make a decision before he or she understands the need to count the cost. Jesus always encouraged people to count the cost. He said in Luke 14:27–28, "And whosoever doth not bear his cross, and come after me, cannot be my disciple. For which of you, intending to build a tower, sitteth not down first, and counteth the cost, whether he have sufficient to finish it?" Then again, Matthew 19 tells the story of the rich young man:

> Good Master, what good thing shall I do, that I may have eternal life?
>
> And he said unto him, Why callest thou me good? there is none good but one, that is, God: but if thou wilt enter into life, keep the commandments.
>
> He saith unto him, Which? Jesus said, Thou shalt do no murder, Thou shalt not commit adultery, Thou shalt not steal, Thou shalt not bear false witness,

> Honour thy father and thy mother: and, Thou shalt love thy neighbour as thyself.
>
> The young man saith unto him, All these things have I kept from my youth up: what lack I yet?
>
> Jesus said unto him, If thou wilt be perfect, go and sell that thou hast, and give to the poor, and thou shalt have treasure in heaven: and come and follow me.
>
> But when the young man heard that saying, he went away sorrowful: for he had great possessions. (Matt. 19:16–22)

Upon witnessing this event, Jesus' disciples were discouraged and asked, "Who then can be saved?"

Jesus reminded them, "The things which are impossible with men are possible with God" (Luke 18:27).

Thank goodness it *is* possible with God, or we would all be lost. Thank goodness Jesus forgives us through *his* perfection, not ours. Even so, we need to be sure our friends and family members know they choose to receive God's love, and they must choose to serve him willingly. We must not lead our friends into an easy faith that does not change their hearts or their lives.

5. Are you ready to invite Jesus into your life and into your heart?

Scripture says in John 1:12, "But as many as received him, to them gave he power to become the sons of God, even to them that believe on his name."

We need to invite, to receive, to accept Jesus into our hearts.

Quiet Please

I am going to give you a couple of key principles. Notice question 5: "Are you ready to invite Jesus into your life and into your heart?"

When you think of question 5, I want you to think of the words *silence* and *pray*. Now as gently as I can, I want to encourage you to change the word *silence* to *shut up*. Shut up is really kind of a nasty, tacky phrase that makes a tremendous point.

Whenever you ask question 5, I would ask you, in love, to *please* shut up!

You have to realize the dynamics that are taking place. The Holy Spirit is working in this one's heart. The angels are rooting for you. The Word of God is applying pressure to this one's very bone and marrow. You, my friend, need to sit in stark silence. Ten seconds of silence to someone under conviction of the power of the Holy Spirit feels like ten minutes. I have seen beads of sweat break out on foreheads as I've waited. But the battle is not with you or me. The battle is with God and his Word. My job, like yours, is to simply take the pages of Scripture, have someone read them out loud, and say, "What does this say to you?" Soon you will ask, "Are you ready to invite Jesus into your heart and into your life?"

When you ask this final question, be silent.

I cannot emphasize how important prayer is at this moment. This could be the height of spiritual warfare. Satan hates what is about to take place. Pray whatever you feel led to pray. Often I look at the person who is doing battle with God and pray in my mind that God will be merciful. I pray Satan will be bound. Yet I do not open my mouth until my lost friend breaks his silence.

Several years ago, I taught this principle to a group of young people. Later, I was enjoying a Broncos football game when one of them called me on the phone. Frank gushed, "Bill, I broke your record."

"What are you talking about?" I asked, my eyes still frozen on John Elway, who was driving toward the goal line.

"You said the longest you ever waited was ten minutes. I talked to this girl, went silent, and sat there for forty-five minutes. My feet got sweaty, and I began to run out of things to pray for."

Now he had my attention. I turned my back to the TV. "What happened?"

"She accepted Christ, of course!"

How long are you willing to wait? When you ask question 5, there are only two possible answers you will hear: yes or no.

When the answer yes comes from a person's heart, this is the precise moment she becomes born again. It's not when she prays the sinner's prayer, walks down the aisle, or performs a ritual; it's the moment she places her faith and trust in the work and person of Jesus Christ. Of course, I'll lead her to pray the sinner's prayer. That's dessert!

You may have your friend or loved one pray a sinner's prayer something like: "Heavenly Father, I have sinned against you. I want forgiveness for all my sins. I believe that Jesus died on the cross for me and rose again. Father, I give you my life to do with as you wish. I want Jesus Christ to come into my life and into my heart. This I ask in Jesus' name. Amen."

What a moment! The joy is rushing, the angels are singing, and your heart is rejoicing in God's goodness. You feel like turning back flips and somersaults.

But what if this moment had turned out differently? What if your friend or loved one had said no? How in the world can you deal with that?

The Why Principle

Whenever I get a no to question 5, I ask, "Why?" The following chapter will again discuss the "Why Principle" as well as other ways to handle objections you might hear when you ask question 5—"Are you ready to invite Jesus into your life and into your heart?"—and receive a no.

Embrace the Unexpected

We mean well. We mean to stop and reach out to others, but we get caught up in life. We stumble over the very blessings God has given us. The blessings of family, hobbies, our job, and our church send us in a mad rush to the fast lane. We get so out of touch, we fail to notice when the Holy Spirit authors the unexpected.

Jesus is unimpressed when we do not take time to follow his leading. We need to pay attention to those people he has put into our path.

"But you don't understand," you may say. "I'm so behind I don't have time to invest my life in sharing the gospel with anyone."

I would argue that when it comes to God's work, you don't have interruptions. You have only divine opportunities. You don't need to worry about maintaining your fast pace. When God gives you the unexpected, he gives you all the time you need. Besides, sharing your faith does not have to be a long-winded affair. Did you know it is possible to share your faith in thirty seconds or less?

You can do it by simply asking the last five "Commitment Questions." I practiced this the first time several years ago. Late one night, I was driving down a dark road. As I rounded a corner, I saw several squad cars with their dome lights blinking. Then I saw a small Volkswagen Beetle crushed against a tree. I could see the hydraulics of the "jaws of life" that had just been used to pull a nineteen-year-old boy out of the mangled car. He lay on a stretcher with IVs jammed into his arms, as the paramedics tried to save his young life.

I pulled over, got out of my car, and made my way to the boy. But I had a problem. A helicopter crew was ready to whisk the boy to the hospital. I had only thirty seconds to share the gospel of Jesus Christ. This was complicated by the fact this boy could not speak. All he could do was groan.

I knelt by his head and whispered, "Are you a sinner?"

"Uhhhh."

"Do you want forgiveness of sins?"

"Uhhhh."

"Do you believe Jesus Christ died on the cross for you and rose again?"

"Uhhhh."

"Are you willing to surrender your life to Jesus Christ?"

"Uhhhh."

"Are you ready to invite Jesus Christ into your life and into your heart?"

"Uhhhh."

You see, if this groan came from the boy's heart, he was saved. The gospel is so simple, it only takes a few seconds to share.

The next day, I read in the paper that the boy died. Yet I know one thing: God loved him enough to give him an opportunity at the last moment to receive his Son Jesus Christ. If that boy did, he is walking the streets of gold saying, "Man, that was close!"

But that's not the end of the story. Seven years later, I conducted a seminar in a small church and told this story. Afterward, a grandmotherly woman approached me. She touched her throat as she softly asked, "Was it a *green* Volkswagen Beetle?"

Nobody knew that but the Lord and me. I said, "Yes, ma'am. How did you know?"

With tears in her eyes she whispered, "That was my grandson."

God loved her enough to let her know that her grandson had one more opportunity to come to him. So when you look back at this story, was the car accident an interruption to my life or a God-given opportunity? Perhaps this will help you look at your own interruptions in a new light.

Keita Andrews is a man who allows life's interruptions to be used by God as opportunities. At 4:30 one morning, I stood in a Denny's restaurant and taught him and a bunch of other UPS drivers how to share their faith.

Keita called me a week later to tell me about all the people he had led to Christ. He was almost flying. He could hardly catch his breath as he told me story after story of how he had led people to the Lord in parks, stores, everywhere.

I said, "I've got to meet you."

We met, I fell completely in love with him, and we became close friends. One day, Keita's life was interrupted. As he jumped out of his UPS truck, his knee collapsed under him. Later, after major surgery, he called me and asked, "Do you know any ministry that pays to share your faith?"

I laughed and said, "If I knew that, I would be in it myself, Keita."

That evening, when my wife came home from her job as a nurse at an inner-city health clinic, she mentioned the clinic was looking for a chaplain.

I immediately called the board of directors and told them about Keita. He got the job.

At that time, this clinic saw more than fifteen thousand people a year. Many of those patients came through Keita's office and heard his questions and read the Scriptures. We have lost count of the number of people who have come to Jesus.

One day, after my wife finished her job at the clinic, she started to walk to her car. A man ran behind her and grabbed her purse. Her first reaction was shock, but her second reaction was to charge. So here's my fifty-plus-year-old wife running down the street, chasing a crack dealer. The mugger ran into a crack house, and my wife pounded on the door and shouted, "If you don't give me my purse, I am going to put Bill and Keita on you."

Later, when she told me the story, I called Keita. He knew the mugger, so we went and sat outside his house. A man in a wheelchair showed up. Keita led him to Christ. Then the man who stole my wife's purse showed up, and Keita led him to Christ. A few days later, the mugger apologized to my wife and returned her purse. Only the money was missing.

Not that I recommend chasing crack dealers down the street, but I do recommend you pay close attention to all the interruptions that come into your life. Give each of them to God and allow him to react through you with his love and power. When you do, you will see God use all things for his good, even bum knees and stolen purses.

Be Thankful

Remember, as you watch for opportunities, God wants you to simply be thankful.

The Holy Spirit wants to use your faithfulness to bless two people, the person you are sharing with as well as yourself. He wants you to experience the joy of Philemon, verse 6, "That the communication of thy faith may become effectual by the acknowledging of every good thing which is in you in Christ Jesus."

Coach Dave Nicholl said, "The summer I began to share my faith with the graduating seniors, I experienced that kind of joy in my heart. My relationship with Christ grew. I was more excited than when I saw the Broncos win the Super Bowl."

The Holy Spirit wants you to experience this joy so you will have a full understanding of what you have in Christ. Through this process, you may be amazed at how God will use you.

Coach Dave adds, "Plug into where God is moving. Take advantage of every opportunity. One night, the phone rang. A phone solicitor from New Mexico was trying to sell me something. I listened to his pitch and told him, 'I'm not interested.' As he tried his pitch a second time, I said, 'I have a question for you. Do you have any kind of spiritual belief?' That's when I learned something. God is moving, not just in Windsor, Colorado, but all over the world. I was elated when the salesman gave his heart to Christ."

Test every opportunity that comes your way. When you find God is moving, join him, and like Coach Dave, you will be thankful that your joy is complete.

Review

Commitment questions:

1. Are you a sinner?
2. Do you want forgiveness of sins?
3. Do you believe Jesus Christ died on the cross for you and rose again?
4. Are you willing to surrender your life to Jesus Christ?
5. Are you ready to invite Jesus Christ into your life and into your heart?

After you ask these questions, remember, *be silent and pray!* If your friend says yes to question 5, you may want to lead him through the following prayer: "Heavenly Father, I have sinned against you. I want forgiveness for all my sins. I believe that Jesus died on the cross for me and rose again. Father, I give you my life to do with as you wish. I want Jesus Christ to come into my life and into my heart. This I ask in Jesus' name. Amen."

Remember, you may want to write down these questions as well as this prayer in your Bible. The next chapter will show you how to support the person who has said yes to Jesus.

Chapter 7
WHAT TO DO WHEN SOMEONE RECEIVES CHRIST

The moment someone I am sharing with receives Christ, I try to affirm and confirm what has just happened. I do this because when someone can testify unashamedly about the gospel, she's taken the first step in her new faith walk. For as Scripture says in 1 Corinthians 12:3, "No man can say that Jesus is the Lord but by the Holy Ghost."

We need to encourage the new believer to sign their name in the back of the PWT and note the date of their commitment. Tell them, "By signing here, you are making a commitment to God that you will do your best to follow Jesus Christ."

Next, it is important to have them read the three "Assurance As a Believer" verses below their signature. They should refer to these verses often, especially if they ever begin to question the decision they have made for Christ. Verses such as:

Romans 10:9 – That if thou shalt confess with thy mouth the Lord Jesus, and shalt believe in thine heart that God hath raised him from the dead, thou shalt be saved.

1 John 5:13 – These things have I written unto you that believe on the name of the Son of God; that ye may know that ye have eternal life, and that ye may believe on the name of the Son of God.

Finally, there are some questions and directions we should cover with the new believer.

Just the other night I happened to call Jerry, a friend of mine. Jerry picked up the phone and said, "Bill! There's someone here I want you to meet. Brenda has some exciting news."

As he handed Brenda the phone, I had to chuckle because I knew what was coming. I asked, "Brenda, how are you?"

She said, "I can't hear you. There's too much commotion here."

"Why? What happened?"

"I just gave my life to Jesus!"

"How'd that happen?"

"I felt this emptiness in my life, even though my marriage was going well and my job was great. My girlfriend set up this meeting with Jerry. He had me read some Scriptures out loud, then he kept asking what they meant. That's when I realized how desperately I needed Christ."

"May I ask you a couple of questions?"

Brenda laughed. "You too?"

"How many of your sins has Christ paid for?"

"All of them."

"Do you know how many of your sins God remembers?"

"I think I do. None."

I grinned. "You are absolutely right. Brenda, where does Jesus live?"

Joyfully, she answered, "He lives within my heart!"

What a moment of celebration! Brenda had indeed made a commitment to Christ. But notice, Jerry and I were not about to leave Brenda without following up. To abandon a new believer would be like leaving a baby in a blizzard. We needed to make sure we put Brenda on a path that would lead her to a deeper relationship with the Lord. The first step in helping a new believer start this process is to ask the questions I asked Brenda.

Questions and Directions for a New Believer

As you recall, the first question I asked was:

1. How many sins has Christ paid for?

I asked this because I wanted to make sure she understood, for her sake as well as mine. First John 2:2 says, "And he is the propitiation for our sins: and not for ours only, but also for the sins of the whole world." It is clear Christ died for all of us and all our sins.

When I heard her answer, "All!" to my question, I proceeded to the next question.

2. How many of your sins does Christ remember?

Her answer should be, "None." You may want to remind the new believer that the Word, in Hebrews 10:17, says, "And their sins and iniquities will I remember no more."

It is important for the new believer to realize he is a new creation. Second Corinthians 5:17 says, "Therefore if any man be in Christ, he is a new creature: old things are passed away; behold, all things are become new."

3. Where does Christ live?

The answer we are looking for is "within me." Galatians 2:20 says, "I am crucified with Christ: nevertheless I live; yet not I, but Christ liveth in me."

This is an important concept, and I want to be sure the new believer understands he or she has a relationship with Christ. I follow this question with another.

4. Let's pray.

I love to teach a new believer how to talk with God. I tell him, "Just say, 'Heavenly Father,' then tell him what's on your heart. When you're done say, 'I ask all this in Jesus' name.'"

I have heard prayers last ten seconds to ten minutes. The length doesn't matter. What matters is that the process of prayer has begun.

5. Who has been praying for you?

I always ask a new believer, "Who has been praying for you?"

I find that 95 percent of the time she knows. She usually tells me it was her mother, father, grandmother, friend, coworker, family member, or schoolmate. I next ask:

6. Do you know where your friend goes to church?

I ask this because I want to affirm that the new believer's praying friend or family member goes to a Bible-based church and is a Bible-based Christian. If I find this to be so, I say:

7. Do you know your friend's phone number? Let's call him now!

If a telephone is convenient, I ask, "Do you have the phone number?"

We dial up that person right then. My friend, usually through tears, says something like, "I just thought I'd call and tell you I've just given my life to Jesus."

Frequently, there is much rejoicing on the other end of the phone. This, of course, is one of the main reasons I have the new believer call. I'm trying to give joy back to the body of Christ. I want my joy to belong to everyone.

The other reason I have the new believer call is because I want him to share with someone else. I do this because it is important he shares his faith in Jesus Christ with others. For as Romans 10:9 says, "That if thou shalt confess with thy mouth the Lord Jesus, and shalt believe in thine heart that God hath raised him from the dead, thou shalt be saved."

Also, Jesus himself said in Luke 9:26, "For whosoever shall be ashamed of me and of my words, of him shall the Son of man be ashamed, when he shall come in his own glory, and in his Father's, and of the holy angels."

For these reasons alone, it is important to tell the good news of your salvation. Plus, I want my friend to become comfortable sharing what God has done in his life.

Alan is a good example of what can happen when a new believer is encouraged to share his faith. The first thing he did when he became a believer was to contact all three of his children. He went through the whole presentation with each one of them. Then, over the course of the next few weeks, he shared the gospel with a dozen different people!

Even what would have been opportunities for potential temptation he used as an opportunity to share the gospel. When a female friend called to tell him she was thinking about divorcing her husband and hinted she needed his comfort, he turned the conversation around and said, "May I ask you a question? Do you have any spiritual beliefs?"

By sharing his faith, he found this woman was a Christian, and he encouraged her to walk in the right way.

8. May I take you to church?

When your friend accepts Christ as his Savior, one of the most important things he needs to do is to become a part of a church fellowship. Not only is this important to the body of Christ; it is important for his own spiritual growth.

I met Holly several years ago. She had received Christ, and I had set her up with a good church under a good pastor. A few months later, she called me sobbing. "I'm in so much trouble; I'm eating out of a dumpster."

I immediately called her pastor, and we met with Holly. As we talked, she turned her life back to Jesus. Thank goodness Holly had the support of a good pastor and a church that could reach out to her and help her get back on her feet.

A couple of years ago, I saw another example of a church and pastor making a difference in the lives of new believers. One Sunday morning after I preached, Carlton answered the altar call. The pastor and I did not realize he was there to give his life to Christ, because he was lost in a crowd gathered to repent from the sin of silence.

Carlton's new faith walk did not have an easy start. That afternoon his fiancée saw him talking with another woman. She pulled off her engagement ring and left the restaurant in tears. That night, Carlton came back to the seminar, a whipped puppy. He told the pastor, "I want to be committed to my new faith in Christ, but my life is falling apart."

The first thing the pastor did was to clarify. "Do you really want God's will in your life? If you do, you will have to quit living with your fiancée."

Carlton agreed to move out of Gail's apartment. The pastor helped him find another place to live and began to disciple him, meeting with him for prayer and Bible study. Gail couldn't help but notice Carlton's change of lifestyle and heart. Impressed, she listened to the pastor present the gospel and also received Christ as her Savior. Soon after, the pastor had the privilege of marrying Carlton and Gail in a simple ceremony. The bride's and groom's faces glowed with wedding day joy, which mingled with the joy of following Christ in obedience. Today, this couple is growing together in the Lord and reaching back to tell others the good news of Jesus Christ.

What a beautiful example of a church and pastor supporting a new believer. Your friend will also need support from the body of Christ. If your friend lives near you, you may ask, "May I take you to church?"

Please follow through with your offer. Pick up your friend for church the very next Sunday. This will help remove his fear of the unknown. Once at church, introduce your friend to the pastor. It is an honor to disciple a new believer in this way. You will be able to watch his joy grow as his faith deepens.

If your friend lives far away or can't attend your church, ask, "Would you feel more comfortable in a small or large church?"

You may have to do some research, but with a few phone calls you can find a Bible-believing church in his area that matches his preference for church size. If he has no preference, give him the name of a Bible-believing church near his home. Also, give your friend the name and number of the pastor.

Because I sometimes introduce a person to Christ when I'm out of town, visiting another city, I'm often not the one who gets to take this new believer to church for the first time. But that's OK because I can still help him start the process of finding a church home. Here's what I do:

- I locate a church in his area that I think would be good.
- I call the pastor and give him my friend's name and number.
- I ask the pastor to call my friend. I don't care who calls whom first, just as long as a call is made. But while I have the pastor on the phone, my job is to get him to promise me that either he or someone he designates will call my friend. I ask him to call, not only to give the times of the church services, but to agree to have someone meet my friend at the front door, answer his questions, and help him get involved in Sunday school or a small group. It is only then that I have peace of mind.
- Twenty-four hours later, I call the pastor back to make sure he has made the promised arrangements.

So as you can see, even if you live far away from your friend, you can follow this procedure to help your friend find a church home.

9. Read the Gospel of John.

Soon after my friend becomes a believer, I give him an assignment, just as I gave to Brenda that night. I say, "I promise that when you read the Gospel of John tonight, it will seem different to you."

Rereading the Word will seem different to a new believer because now it has meaning, whereas before it did not.

I want to make sure the new believer follows through with this assignment, so I say something like:

10. I will call you tomorrow to see if the Word became different.

Call back in a day or two to see if your friend has fulfilled your request. When he has, ask, "Did the Bible seem different?"

When he answers yes, say, "It may seem different, but the book didn't change. You did. You will start to notice other changes. For example, in the next day or two, you may find that some of the language from your old life may suddenly seem wrong. These are indicators Christ is living in you. You no longer live for yourself, but you live for Christ."

Second Corinthians 5:15 says, "And that he died for all, that they which live should not henceforth live unto themselves, but unto him which died for them, and rose again."

Why Follow Through to Make Disciples?

Why should we continue to do follow-up with the new believer? After all, her decision for Christ has already been made. Aren't we done? No, of course not. For one thing, Jesus commanded us to make *disciples*. Matthew 28:19–20 says, "Go ye therefore, and teach all nations, baptizing them in the name of the Father, and of the Son, and of the Holy Ghost: Teaching them to observe all things whatsoever I have commanded you: and, lo, I am with you alway, even unto the end of the world. Amen."

What is a disciple? First, a disciple is a born-again believer. And second, a disciple needs to grow in his relationship with Christ.

Think of it this way, the new believer is much like a baby. She needs a lot of care and feeding. Her growth to adulthood will come from time spent in prayer, reading God's Word, fellowship, worship, and service.

We have a responsibility to provide everything the new believer needs in order to grow.

My friend Jerry understands this principle. That is why he followed up and made sure that Brenda found a good Bible-believing church. Brenda's journey has just started. As she grows in her faith, she will find God's comfort and care as well as his guidance in the midst of life's best and toughest circumstances. What an exciting journey Brenda has ahead of her! And the greatest thing is now she is no longer alone.

In the next chapter, we will review how to respond to the thirty-six most common objections.

Review

After your friend comes to the Lord, ask the following questions. You may want to write these new believer questions and directions in your Bible as well:

1. How many sins has Christ paid for?
2. How many of your sins does Christ remember?
3. Where does Christ live?
4. Let's pray. *(The new believer should say what's on his heart.)*
5. Who has been praying for you?
6. Do you know where your friend goes to church?
7. Do you know your friend's phone number? Let's call him now!
8. May I take you to church with me?
9. Read the Gospel of John.
10. I will call you tomorrow to see if the Word became different.

Chapter 8

READY RESPONSES TO COMMON OBJECTIONS

The best way to conquer an objection is through a simple three-letter word, the question "Why?" When someone says, "I am not ready," don't second-guess his reason. Instead, do what a psychologist does. Many folks are willing to pay a psychologist a hundred bucks an hour just so he can ask, "Why do you feel this way?" The psychologist asks, "Why?" because he doesn't presume to know until he's been told.

The "Why Principle" will work for us. Never assume you know the reason why a person is not ready to accept Christ. Instead, ask, "Why?" It is the only way to get your friend to burp up his real issues.

Here's how it works:

You: Are you ready to invite Jesus Christ into your life?

Friend: No.

You: Why?

Friend: I'm not ready.

You: Why?

Now that you've asked "Why?" your friend may come up with the real issue. For example, he may say, "My wife will leave me," "I like to party," or "I'll lose my friends." These are issues you can deal with once you know what they are. Plus, when your friend voices his real reason aloud, it may sound dumb, even to him.

I remember a time the "Why Principle" worked in this way. I was talking with a man who said, "I am not ready to receive Jesus Christ." I asked, "Why?"

He made some confusing remarks about his business affairs, and when he finished speaking, he looked at me and said, "That doesn't make any sense, does it?"

I said, "Nope. Are you ready to give your life to Christ?" He was and he did!

Once you discover your friend's real objection, never fall into the temptation to argue. Don't be motivated by a desire to be right or to prove him wrong. Instead, be motivated to share Jesus in love. As the saying goes, "It is impossible to express love with a clenched fist or stinging arguments." So remember to stay cool; ask, "Why?"; and listen to your friend's objections. This is one of the best ways you can demonstrate your love for him as well as for God.

The Most Common Objections

In this section, you will find a discussion of the responses to thirty-six of the most common objections I've heard. Don't worry about memorizing these responses; instead, read and study them so you'll be prepared. Scripture says, "But sanctify the Lord God in your hearts: and be ready always to give an answer to every man that asketh you a reason of the hope that is in you with meekness and fear" (1 Pet. 3:15).

The "Where to Find Help" section in the front of the PWT offers a wealth of information when handling objections. You will find passages dealing with more than one hundred topics such as "Anxiety," "Discouragement," "Temptation," "Forgiveness," and "Freedom." It is very helpful for an unbeliever to see this. Often they only see the Bible as a book of condemnation. This section will help them realize that the Bible was designed to help them.

The following is a list of the ten most common of the thirty-six objections I've encountered. The number printed at the end of each objection is the location of its corresponding response in this chapter as well as in appendix 2.

1. I'm not ready. (18)
2. My friends will think I'm crazy if I accept Jesus. (24)
3. What about my family? (32)
4. I've done too many bad things. (21)
5. I'm having too much fun. (14)
6. Why does God let bad things happen? (34)
7. There are many paths to God. (27)
8. There are many religions in the world. (28)
9. I've always believed in God. (20)
10. There are too many hypocrites in the church. (31)

The following thirty-six objections and their responses are listed in alphabetical order. For a complete list of all thirty-six objections, as well as thirty-six quick reference response scripts, see appendix 2.

1. A Christian hurt me.

Jeannie said, "All the Christians I know are rude and are in my face trying to convert me. When I don't respond the way they want, it ruins our friendship. I feel they look down on me."

When I hear something like this, I say, "I'm so sorry that happened. Would you accept my apology for those who did that to you?"

Please notice, I have no way to know if her perception is valid, but that doesn't matter because to her it's real. So, when I get below the surface to her hurt, I say, "I am so sorry if your father was a legalist or some Christian was angry and shoved the gospel in your face. I would like to apologize for them. Jesus would not have wanted that to have happened to you."

I sometimes say to Jeannie or someone like her, "Have you ever tried to love somebody and made a mess out of it? You had good intentions, but everything went wrong. Do you think there was a possibility in your friend's desire for you to know Jesus that she just went about it the wrong way?"

Do you notice I always ask questions? I never argue. Also, when you give someone permission to be hostile, the hostility will go away. She may say, "You may be right about my friend, but some Christians seem so narrow and angry."

"You know," I say, "you and Jesus are already in agreement on one thing. He doesn't like that behavior either. By the way, what is your understanding of who Jesus is?"

2. Cults are the answer?

Cult members are easy to spot because they deny the deity of Jesus Christ, plus they teach that you have to earn salvation. Still, it can be hard to discern what they believe because they often engage in double talk. That means they assign alternate meanings to Christian terminology to gain your trust.

When you do meet someone who is involved in a cult, don't try to start a debate. Ask the direct question, "If what you are believing is not true, would you want to know?"

One morning, as I was getting ready to go out, I saw a lady with a briefcase and a ten-year-old boy standing at my door. I knew immediately they were Jehovah's Witnesses. I was running late, but I didn't want to miss an opportunity to share.

When I answered the door, the woman said, "Hello, I'm from the Watchtower."

I said, "If what you believe is not true, would you want to know?"

"What I believe is true, and I'm here to give you that truth."

I asked again. "If what you are believing is not true, would you want to know it?"

"I know the truth."

It took twelve tries before she finally admitted, "Yes, I do want to know."

She's visited me twice so far, and I'm still sharing with her.

Another question I ask is, "Who is Jesus Christ?"

Usually the cult member responds, "He was a good teacher."

I ask, "Do good teachers lie?"

"Good ones don't."

"Isn't it interesting that Jesus said he was God?"

At the back of my Bible, I list the references of several Scriptures that point to Christ's deity. I open my Bible and show them. It would be a good idea to reference these Scriptures in the back of your Bible as well:

- "I and my Father are one" (John 10:30). The literal translation of this means Jesus and the Father are of the same essence.
- "If ye had known me, ye should have known my Father also: and from henceforth ye know him, and have seen him" (John 14:7).
- "I am Alpha and Omega, the beginning and the ending, saith the Lord, which is, and which was, and which is to come, the Almighty" (Rev. 1:8). We know this was Jesus speaking in Revelation 1:8 for the book closes with:
- "He which testifieth these things saith, Surely I come quickly. Amen. Even so, come, Lord Jesus" (Rev. 22:20).
- Also, the following makes a convincing point: "Who is the image of the invisible God, the firstborn of every creature: For by him were all things created, that are in heaven, and that are in earth, visible and invisible, whether they be thrones, or dominions, or principalities, or powers: all things were created by him, and for him" (Col. 1:15–16).
- "Before Abraham was, I am" (John 8:58). The Jewish people knew Jesus was referring to himself as God when he called himself "I am!" He was referring to the divine name of God found in Exodus 3:14. "God said unto Moses, I AM THAT I AM: and he said, Thus shalt thou say unto the children of Israel, I AM hath sent me unto you" (Exod. 3:14).

- "Therefore the Jews sought the more to kill him, because he not only had broken the sabbath, but said also that God was his Father, making himself equal with God" (John 5:18).

I also take cult members to a couple of verses that demonstrate how Jesus allowed worship of himself.

- "And he said, Lord, I believe. And he worshipped him" (John 9:38).
- "And Thomas answered and said unto him, My Lord and my God. Jesus saith unto him, Thomas, because thou hast seen me, thou hast believed: blessed are they that have not seen, and yet have believed" (John 20:28–29).
- "And again, when he bringeth in the firstbegotten into the world, he saith, And let all the angels of God worship him" (Heb. 1:6).

Next I ask, "Did Jesus ever sin? No? You are right. He never sinned in either thought or deed."

- "For we have not an high priest which cannot be touched with the feeling of our infirmities; but was in all points tempted like as we are, yet without sin" (Heb. 4:15).

I tell the cult member, "He is the sin bearer for you and for me. He taught us to worship the Lord God only. Why did Jesus allow worship of himself unless he never sinned?"

I also ask, "Who can forgive sin but God alone? If Jesus were not God, how could he forgive sin and not sin himself?"

- "And, behold, they brought to him a man sick of the palsy, lying on a bed: and Jesus seeing their faith said unto the sick of the palsy; Son, be of good cheer; thy sins be forgiven thee. . . . But that ye may know that the Son of man hath power on earth to forgive sins, (then saith he to the sick of the palsy,) Arise, take up thy bed, and go unto thine house. And he arose, and departed to his house" (Matt. 9:2, 6–7).

Even in the face of this evidence, some cult members may have trouble understanding that God is both God the Father and God the Son. Recently, Linda met a Jehovah's Witness and his young son at her front door. Linda explained to the dad, "You are both a son and a father. Although you have the different roles of being both a son and a father, you are the same person. Much like you, God is both God the Son and God the Father, at the same time. He has different roles, but he is the same person."

Linda reports, "At this explanation, I could see a small light blink on. They didn't respond, but I pray that they will someday be open to the gospel."

If I can get a concession that Jesus is God, then we are off and running with the "Share Jesus Presentation." You may also want to see the Scripture references under objection 17, "I'm not good enough," to complete the presentation.

Often, when cult members knock at your door, they come in teams of two adults, one senior and one junior. The junior is most likely in training. I always focus on the junior. At the end of our time together, I give both members my phone number. That way, if the senior wants to talk to me later, in private, he can call me, as can the junior.

Also, note that Jehovah's Witnesses are not allowed to pray with you or take your literature because they consider you an infidel. When I invite them and other cult members to sit with me, I say, "Whenever I open my Bible, I always pray first." Then I bow my head and pray out the entire gospel. Their eyes may be open, but so are their ears. In this way I can present the gospel in its entirety without interruption.

Even if you are not an expert on what a particular cult believes, you can be most effective when you share your testimony and gently point to the fact Jesus is Lord. But remember, we are a body, and God has created different gifts within the body. You may simply be the qualifier or the one who initiates the conversation with questions and Scriptures. If you get "stuck," don't be afraid to ask a friend, pastor, or "expert" for help. You may be giving him a chance to exercise his gift in leading cult members to the Lord. I have done this myself with wonderful results.

3. God cannot forgive me.

Often I hear, "God cannot forgive me."

When I hear this objection, I turn to Romans 10:13, "For whosoever shall call upon the name of the Lord shall be saved," and ask the person I'm sharing with to read it aloud.

I can remember sitting in a booth with a man in a restaurant who said, "God can't possibly forgive me for all I have done. I've ruined my family, my life, and hurt so many people."

I turned to Romans 10:13 and said, "Read it out loud."

He did. I asked, "What does it say to you?"

He started to tremble.

"Look," I said, "does it say God will forgive a repentant murderer?"

"Yes."

"Will he forgive a bank robber?"

"Yes."

"Can he forgive a man who trashed his marriage and hurt other people?"

To my surprise, this man shouted, "I can be forgiven!" Then he put his head on the table and wept. A few moments later, we held hands while he prayed the sinner's prayer, asking God to forgive him of all his sins and asking Christ into his life.

4. How can a loving God send someone to hell?

Our culture often does not have a sensitivity to what sin is because moral absolutes are seldom taught in school. Somehow, we have become convinced God will not send someone to hell. That is the easiest thing in all of Scripture to prove wrong. We begin by looking at the cross. The cross demonstrates the love of God, a love that nailed Jesus to the cross for the sins of the world. This one selfless act demonstrates the depth of God's perfect love in order to reconcile man to himself.

But we also need to talk about the other message of the cross, the perfect justice of God. You see, Jesus Christ never committed a sin in thought, word, or deed. Yet on the cross, Jesus became the sin bearer. Psalms says Christ would cry out, "My God, my God, why hast thou forsaken me? why art thou so far from helping me, and from the words of my roaring?" (Ps. 22:1).

This Scripture tells us that when Jesus Christ became our sin bearer, God turned his back on him. God heaped all of his waves of wrath upon his own Son. This is a picture of God's perfect justice. Even one sin separates us from God—no exception. This is why Jesus died in our place. If this were not the case, don't you think that God would have spared his own Son?

5. How can I know the Bible is true?

As we have discussed in an earlier chapter, God has promised us not one crossed *t* or dotted *i* has come about by the will of man.

I spend a lot of time evangelizing the staff in a certain restaurant chain in my area. I remember one day a nonbelieving waiter named Danny saw me as I was seated at my table. Danny dropped by and said, "Bill, we have a new guy I'd like you to meet. His name is Art, and he likes statistics."

I chuckled. "Go get him."

So there was Danny, a nonbeliever, bringing another nonbeliever to my table as if he's delivering a pizza, just so I could share the gospel. What a sense of humor God has!

Soon Art, a six-foot-six-inch guy with Coke-bottle glasses, walked over. I decided to put a question into a conversation to see if God was at work. I said, "Art, I understand you like statistics."

"Yes."

"What is a penny doubled every day, for thirty days?"

Art spouted off, "It starts at 1, 2, 4, 8, 16, 32, 64, 128, 256, until you get $10,737,418.24."

I was impressed! I said, "That seemed easy for you. Let me ask you another question. How many people would it take flipping a quarter before one person hits heads thirty times in a row?"

Art ran into the kitchen. When he came back, he said it would take billions of people flipping quarters before one person hit heads thirty times in a row. Art's right. According to *Ripley's Believe It or Not! Strange Coincidences,*[1] for a tossed coin to fall to heads fifty times in a row would require one million men tossing ten coins a minute for forty hours a week—and then it would occur only once in every nine centuries.

With this probability established, I was ready to make the switch. I said, "That is why I believe the Bible is true. If you take the thirty prophecies about the birth, the death, and the resurrection of Jesus that have come true, that's like flipping heads thirty times in a row."

Art froze. I said, "I don't want to take time away from your work, but as you go back to your station today, think about this: how many people would it take flipping a quarter before one person hits heads 245 times? I picked that number because it is a conservative estimate of the number of biblical prophecies that were supposed to come true that have come true."

Stunned, Art asked, "Can we make an appointment?"

"I'd be glad to."

I'm happy to say, a few days later I met with Art, and the angels rejoiced at his decision to follow Christ.

The other day I asked a friend what the odds were of 245 prophecies coming true. He said, "Bill, the odds would be a billion to one." To me that figures to a God who is sovereign and powerful with infinity behind him.

6. How do I know I have enough faith?

When someone tells me he is afraid he doesn't have enough faith to receive Christ as his Savior, I smile and say, "If you have enough faith to ask Christ to come into your heart, you have enough faith to receive him into your heart. Imagine Moses. As he led his people out of Egypt, he met a pretty big roadblock—the Red Sea. As Pharaoh's army closed in on Moses and the tribes of Israel, God directed him to cross the sea. Moses stood on the shore, wondering if he had enough faith. It wasn't until he put his foot in the water that the sea parted. God will honor your first step. If you really want to know Jesus as Lord, take the first step and ask him into your heart."

7. I can't live the Christian lifestyle.

At this I say, "I am so glad you understand a change is required. But unlike the past, you are not going to have to change alone. The Bible says in Philippians 4:13, 'I can do all things through Christ which strengtheneth me.'

"God wants your 'want to,' not your ability. He wants your desire. Are you desiring now to follow Jesus Christ as your Lord?"

If your friend says yes, it is time for the sinner's prayer.

8. I don't believe in God.

This objection usually comes up only at the beginning of the "Share Jesus Presentation." When it does, I ask, "May I show you the Scriptures that changed my life?" I like to show the Scriptures because I find the Holy Spirit often moves their hearts to belief.

Yet sometimes this question will surface at the end of the presentation. When it does, I say, "If you became convinced that God existed, would you be willing to give your life to him?"

If the person answers yes, I ask, "Would you be willing to ask a nonexistent God to help you in your unbelief?"

We pray together, "God, if you are real, help me to believe."

I tell him to see what happens in the next week or month. We set a date to meet again in a few weeks. While I'm waiting for the meeting, I pray for truth to be revealed in his life.

This reminds me of the time a few years ago when I was being interviewed by a Colorado Springs newspaper, and the reporter, Mr. Gray, wanted to do an article about my life before I met Christ. He was fascinated by the fact that I was visiting jails and prisons and sharing my faith instead of being locked up in one.

Mr. Gray took me into a big boardroom, just the two of us, and we were seated in overstuffed leather chairs. I had brought my big Bible along because if he took my picture, I wanted the cross on my Bible to show what had changed my life.

Mr. Gray said, "Let's get something straight, Mr. Fay. I don't believe in God, so don't even try to convert me."

I smiled. "I couldn't convert you if I wanted."

He picked up his pen. "By the way, how *do* you convert people?"

It was all I could do to keep from laughing because I knew I was watching my Father at work. I said, "I generally ask five questions."

"What are the questions?"

When I got about halfway through, he stopped me and said, "You're trying to convert me."

So I stopped asking the "Share Jesus Questions" and proceeded with the interview. He grilled me for an hour and a half. As the interview wound down, I felt it was my chance to get even. With my most pleasant expression, I said, "May I have permission to show you the seven verses of Scripture that changed my life?"

Notice I did not barge ahead; I asked permission. Mr. Gray had to be a real stinker to say no to my request, considering what he had just put me through. When he said yes, I had him read the Scriptures out loud, then I asked him what they said to him. I watched his facade start to melt as the power of God began to do its work.

He did not accept Christ as his Savior that day, but we still see each other from time to time. The last time I saw him, he said, "I can still remember those verses." He hasn't yet surrendered his life. But God may not be finished with him. My point is, always be ready to share the Scripture, yet never force the issue.

9. I don't believe the Resurrection took place.

Whenever I find someone who holds this belief, I say, "I'm glad this is your only stumbling block, because one thing God did for us is to provide overwhelming evidence of the Resurrection. In fact, one of the leading legal minds of the country, Dr. Simon Greenleaf, an outstanding professor of law at Harvard University, wrote a volume in which he examined the legal value of the apostles' testimony to the resurrection of Christ.

"Greenleaf concluded that the resurrection of Christ was one of the best supported events in history, according to the laws of legal evidence administered in courts of justice."[2]

"Did you know Jeremiah 29:13 says, 'And ye shall seek me, and find me, when ye shall search for me with all your heart'? If you want to test your heart right now, why don't you bow your head and pray, 'Lord Jesus, if the Resurrection took place, help me in my unbelief.'"

Also, see the story in the introduction in chapter 6, "Bring to Decision," or see response 9 in appendix 2.

10. I want to think about it.

I remember speaking in a church in a tiny town in northern Colorado. The pastor asked me to stand at the back door of the church and greet people on their way out. A farmer approached me. I asked, "How's your morning?"

"Fine."

"Do you know the Lord?"

"Nope."

I've got this big guy by the hand. He's pulling to go out the door, and I'm pulling to bring him back.

"Sir, why not?"

"I don't know. I guess I want to think about it."

"You heard me preach. If you die, where are you going?"

"Hell."

"Then have a wonderful day, sir."

A few days later, Floyd was knocking at the pastor's door. He couldn't stand it anymore. The idea of hell had become real to him, and he was ready to give his life to Jesus Christ. The pastor called me to celebrate.

11. I'm a good person.

I love the saying "A man who believes in nothing but himself, lives in a very small world."

When someone tells me, "I'm a good person," I politely as possible ask, "By whose standards?"

"What do you mean?"

"Let me give you an example. Have you ever committed murder?"

"No."

"Let's check it out by God's definition. Have you ever been angry, hated, called someone a fool, or waved someone off on the freeway? Because if you have, by God's standards, you are a murderer."

Before she catches her breath, I plow ahead, "Have you ever looked at the opposite sex and lusted?"

I don't give her the chance to answer. I say, "By the way, if you say no, I know you are guilty of lying. By God's standards, if you have lusted, you are guilty of adultery. Have you put a relationship, a job, or some activity that you would rather do or have over a relationship with God? Because if you have, those items became your idols.

"Because of the holiness of God, it is impossible to measure up to his standards of perfection. Since God is the judge and the jury, it is his approval we have to meet. In fact, Scripture says, 'For whosoever shall keep the whole law, and yet offend in one point, he is guilty of all' (James 2:10).

"I want you to know that I, like you, have been guilty as well. The difference is I found forgiveness through Jesus. And that's the forgiveness I am asking you if you want."

12. I'm a member of another world religion.

Here is an example of how I shared my faith with Lee, a young Japanese Buddhist I met at church. She was in the United States to study English and culture. One Sunday morning, I felt led to share my faith with her, but I wanted to do so with respect and love. So I asked her, "Does truth matter to you?"

"Yes."

"I know your family and culture have given you a different set of beliefs than my own. Has anyone told you about Christianity?"

"No, but I would like to know about it."

"Lee, who taught you to tell your first lie?"

"No one."

There I stopped and told her the story of Adam and Eve in the garden of Eden, explained how sin entered into the world, and told her all people have a sin nature.

Surprised, she said, "I have a sin nature too."

I opened my Bible and had her read me the "Share Jesus Scriptures" out loud. When I got to the third verse, I could see she was beginning to understand. But I wanted to be very careful. When she finished, I said, "Lee, I sense you feel afraid of your family."

Lee began to cry, and I didn't push her further. But it was a joyous surprise when she was the first person to answer the altar call at the end of the worship service later that morning.

God, in his infinite wisdom, knew Lee was going forward that morning because he had sent another Japanese believer to the service. This sister had prayed about giving away a dress and a Japanese Bible to someone who needed them. As you can guess, Lee found both the dress and Japanese Bible a perfect fit.

13. I'm God.

Today, many people share the belief that they are God, which comes from Eastern religions. I like to ask them, "I could use a new car. Could you create one for me? Surely an all-powerful God such as you could do that."

Then I recommend they read the following Scriptures aloud. After each Scripture is read, I ask, "What does this say to you?"

- "Thou shalt have no other gods before me" (Exod. 20:3).
- "Who changed the truth of God into a lie, and worshipped and served the creature more than the Creator, who is blessed for ever. Amen" (Rom. 1:25).
- "Who hath delivered us from the power of darkness, and hath translated us into the kingdom of his dear Son: In whom we have redemption through his blood, even the forgiveness of sins: Who is the image of the invisible God,

> the firstborn of every creature: For by him were all things created, that are in heaven, and that are in earth, visible and invisible, whether they be thrones, or dominions, or principalities, or powers: all things were created by him, and for him: And he is before all things, and by him all things consist" (Col. 1:13–17).

You will also want to point out that this Scripture shows that God is God alone. He is not all things; he is the Creator who holds all things together. You can also say, "I am not God, but he is in me. Would you like God to be in you?"

14. I'm having too much fun.

What are you going to say to the person who says, "I'm having too much fun"?

Again, go back to the "Why Principle." You are going to say, "Why?"

The response will most likely be something like, "I like to party."

When I get this response, I say something like, "In other words, you are into the party scene—sex, drugs, and rock and roll?"

Usually, the person blushes.

I say, "I have one last question. Let's imagine you reject Jesus Christ today, but this weekend you become a part of the interstate highway. Where does the Bible say you will go?"

(*Notice that I always use Scripture. The Bible is my authority, whether he believes it or not.*)

He usually whispers, "I will go to hell."

Then I say, with all the love I can, "Have a nice day and drive carefully."

These people usually do drive carefully for the next forty-eight hours. But I say this not to only remind them of their mortality; I say this hoping they will let the message of God's love and truth penetrate their heads and hearts. I'm not trying to be judgmental, but to prepare them, in the next few moments, days, weeks, or years, to accept Jesus Christ as their Lord and Savior.

15. I'm Jewish.

When someone says, "I can't believe in Jesus," I ask, "Why?" For you see, the issue is not whether he can or can't; it's whether he will or won't. For when it comes to the whole issue of who Jesus is, Josh McDowell, the author of *More Than a Carpenter,* points out the fact that we have only three choices. He says, "Jesus is either Lord, liar, or lunatic."[3]

The first thing I do with the Jewish person is to try to find out if he or she is culturally Jewish or religiously Jewish. I ask, "Do you go to synagogue?"

Most of the time, I get a no for an answer. Then I say, "I believe Jesus is the Christ, who he claimed to be. I know he is not a liar because he never sinned. He's obviously not a lunatic because his life and teachings show he was brilliant, stable, and loving toward others. Therefore, I can only believe that he is Lord. For in his own words, 'I and my Father are one' (John 10:30).

"Also, the Jews of the day clearly knew who Jesus claimed to be because when he said in John 8:58, 'Jesus said unto them, Verily, verily, I say unto you, Before Abraham was, I am. Then took they up stones to cast at him.'

"The Jews knew he was quoting God to Moses, when God said, 'I AM THAT I AM: and he said, Thus shalt thou say unto the children of Israel, I AM hath sent me unto you'" (Exod. 3:14).

I like to point out Christ's identity. It is a great way to take this big issue and turn it into a smaller denominator. For if we can establish that Jesus is truly Jehovah God, the rest comes easy.

If I meet a Jewish person who is religiously Jewish, the first thing I do is remind him that Judaism is the root of my Christianity. Of course, the difficult points for Jews are first, believing Jesus is the Messiah, and second, that he rose from the dead. I say, "If either of these points were true, would you consider having a personal relationship with Jesus to complete your Jewishness?"

Often, I invite the Jewish person to visit a messianic congregation. This way, the worship will seem familiar, and he will hear the testimony of other Jewish people who found Jesus to be the true Messiah.

Remember when I asked my friend if he went to synagogue anywhere? That's because I want to make a distinction as to whether I am talking with a cultural Jew or a practicing Jew. If I am talking to a practicing Jew, I continue the presentation at this point by asking, "Have you ever wondered about the fact that Jesus claimed to be God?"

Then I take him to Isaiah 53 and have him read verses 1–12 aloud.

> Who hath believed our report? and to whom is the arm of the LORD revealed? For he shall grow up before him as a tender plant, and as a root out of a dry ground: he hath no form nor comeliness; and when we shall see him, there is no beauty that we should desire him. He is despised and rejected of men; a man of sorrows, and acquainted with grief: and we hid as it were our faces from him; he was despised, and we esteemed him not. Surely he hath borne our griefs, and carried our sorrows: yet we did esteem him stricken, smitten of God, and afflicted. But he was wounded for our transgressions, he was bruised for our iniquities: the chastisement of our peace was upon him; and with his stripes we are healed. All we like sheep have gone astray; we have turned every one to his own way; and the LORD hath laid on him the iniquity of us all. He was oppressed, and he was afflicted, yet he opened not his mouth: he is brought as a lamb to the slaughter, and as a sheep before her shearers is dumb, so he openeth not his mouth. He was taken from prison and from judgment: and who shall declare his generation? for he was cut off out of the land of the living: for the transgression of my people was he stricken. And he made his grave with the wicked, and with the rich in his death; because he had done no violence, neither was any deceit in his mouth. Yet it pleased the LORD to bruise him; he hath put him to grief: when thou shalt make his soul an offering for sin, he shall see his seed, he shall prolong his days, and the pleasure of the LORD shall prosper in his hand. He shall see of the travail

> of his soul, and shall be satisfied: by his knowledge shall my righteous servant justify many; for he shall bear their iniquities. Therefore will I divide him a portion with the great, and he shall divide the spoil with the strong; because he hath poured out his soul unto death: and he was numbered with the transgressors; and he bare the sin of many, and made intercession for the transgressors.

I ask him, "Who do you think this describes?"

I also ask, "Why do you think many synagogues refuse to read this chapter of Isaiah?"

Then I ask another question that is difficult yet thought provoking: "Do you know why the sacrifices have stopped in the temple?" I wait for his answer, then continue, "Could it be because Jesus is God's sacrificial lamb?"

I don't push. My goal is to have a warm, friendly discussion that will lead to other discussions. If he indicates an interest in learning more, I invite him to meet with a local Messianic pastor—who is far more of an Old Testament expert than I. A fellow Jew will be very sensitive to my friend's culture and feelings.

When it comes to sharing Christ with someone of the Jewish faith, I see myself as a qualifier, a filter, and I am free to turn over my friend to an expert. You should feel free as well to call upon a local Jewish pastor or other Jewish believer for help.

If I determine my friend does not attend synagogue and is what I call a "secular" Jew, then I take him through the same Scriptures about Christ found in my response to objection 2, "Cults are the answer?"

16. I'm not a sinner.

Sometimes when you are sharing the "Share Jesus Scriptures" and you turn to Romans 3:23, "For all have sinned . . . ," your friend may respond by saying something like:

Friend: I haven't committed sins. I've never murdered, stolen, or done other dramatic things that are obviously sin.

You: *(Don't argue or try to explain sin. Instead, turn to Matthew 22:37.)* Read this aloud.

Friend: *(Reading:)* "Thou shalt love the Lord thy God with all thy heart, and with all thy soul, and with all thy mind."

You: Have you ever loved God with all your heart, soul, mind, and strength?

Friend: No.

You: That's what sin is.

17. I'm not good enough.

This objection is a lot like "God cannot forgive me." Yet my response is different. For example, when I hear this objection, the first thing I say is, "Why?" After I listen, I say, "That's one thing we have in common. We are not good enough. This is a problem. There are only two ways to get to heaven: either we have to be perfect, never once committing a sin in word, deed, or thought, or we have to become born again.

"I can become born again by accepting in my heart the finished work and person of Jesus Christ, who paid the penalty for my sins. He has the power to forgive me because of his birth, death, and resurrection. When I believe on him and accept his forgiveness, only then can he erase the sins I have committed in the past. Personally, I opt to choose his forgiveness because I can never be good enough to obtain perfection."

Ephesians 2:8–9 says, "For by grace are ye saved through faith; and that not of yourselves: it is the gift of God: Not of works, lest any man should boast."

I love taking a person with this objection to Romans 10:9–10: "That if thou shalt confess with thy mouth the Lord Jesus, and shalt believe in thine heart that God hath raised him from the dead, thou shalt be saved. For with the heart man believeth unto righteousness; and with the mouth confession is made unto salvation."

Next, I show my friend verse 13, which reads, "For whosoever shall call upon the name of the Lord shall be saved."

I ask, "Does that include you?"

Then I let the power of Scripture speak.

18. I'm not ready.

If your friend tells you she is not ready, ask, "Why?"

More than likely, her reason will sound silly and illogical, even to her. In this case say, "Are you really willing to let that stand between you and God?"

This may be all you need to say to take care of her objection. If she indicates she is now ready to invite Christ into her life, then lead her in prayer.

Then again, her objection may not be so easy to get rid of. For example, in response to your "Why not?" your friend may say something like, "I am not ready because this information is so new to me. This is a whole new way of thinking, and I want to count the cost."

If you get this response, stop the presentation. Be prepared to release your friend to God's sovereignty and control. Say something like, "I enjoyed our time, and I will be praying for you. May I talk to you again in a few days or weeks?"

In this way, you've not put undue pressure on her, and you may gain permission to speak with her in the future. You do not want to harvest a false decision for Christ.

As you part, do not go away feeling like a failure. You may have planted the seed that by God's grace will sprout at a later time. In the meantime, keep your friend in your prayers and look for other opportunities to share with her again.

Be humbled and thankful you did not fail in your outreach with her. You were obedient to Christ, and as long as she has breath, there is hope she will someday be ready to make a decision for him.

19. I'm not sure I'm saved.

Sometimes you will meet someone who has genuinely asked Christ into his heart but feels he is not saved. When I meet someone like this, I point to his watch and say, "That's a very nice watch. If you lost it, you'd miss it when you wanted to see the time. But if you've never owned a watch, you wouldn't worry about looking at it, nor would you worry about losing it.

"Don't you find it interesting that you are worried you are not saved? You can't worry about losing something you don't have. I bet before you asked Christ into your life, you didn't go around worrying that Christ was not in your heart. It is a wonderful confirmation to me that you might be saved because you are concerned.

"Let's look at Romans 8:38–39: 'For I am persuaded, that neither death, nor life, nor angels, nor principalities, nor powers, nor things present, nor things to come, Nor height, nor depth, nor any other creature, shall be able to separate us from the love of God, which is in Christ Jesus our Lord.'"

I ask, "What does this say to you?"

Then I turn to Ephesians 1:13–14 and have him read: "In whom ye also trusted, after that ye heard the word of truth, the gospel of your salvation: in whom also after that ye believed, ye were sealed with that holy Spirit of promise, Which is the earnest of our inheritance until the redemption of the purchased possession, unto the praise of his glory."

I say, "I just want you to know, my friend, the moment you invited Christ in your life, you were saved. God guarantees that one day you will be with him in heaven.

"The fears you have are also experienced by most Christians. But you must move past these fears so you can grow in your faith. You may find it helps to strengthen your faith by reading your Bible, praying, and spending time with other believers. Let me help you get started. May I pick you up for church next Sunday?"

20. I've always believed in God.

When I hear this, I like to say, "The devil believes in God, and in fact, he has even seen God. James 2:19 says, 'Thou believest that there is one God; thou doest well: the devils also believe, and tremble.'"

I ask, "How are you any different? Would you like to receive Jesus as your Savior?"

21. I've done too many bad things.

See "I'm not good enough," response 17, in this chapter.

22. I've tried it and it didn't work out.

The first thing I try to affirm is whether the person is saved or unsaved. I ask, "Tried what?"

After all, I don't know what he tried. Did he try walking down the aisle or singing a song? I want him to tell me.

He usually says something like, "I tried that prayer once, you know, the one where you invite Christ into your life. Nothing happened."

I look him in the eye and say, "Apparently that is very true. Let me ask you a question. Did you mean the prayer when you said it?"

Sixty percent of the time, people will say, "Well, I think so," yet they seem unsure.

Next I ask, "Tell me about that moment you gave your life to Christ."

You may be surprised at how ridiculous their "testimonies" may seem. For example, I remember being with a pastor of a mainline denomination. Now you can't ask a pastor if he is saved, so I said, "Pastor, tell me, how did you first come to find a relationship with God?"

He said, "Son, I was driving down the road one day and heard birds chirping, and I knew then, I knew God."

If that is a testimony that bears with his spirit, then something is wrong. In other words, does your friend have a testimony that bears witness to what Scripture teaches? If not, say, "Can you look into the face of God and tell him you are born again?"

If he says no, say, "Let's take a minute and review the Scriptures. Read them aloud, then tell me what they mean." But *if he says yes,* ask permission to review the seven "Share Scriptures" then ask him the five "Commitment Questions" to help him have a better understanding of the gospel.

23. My beliefs are private.

The first question I ask is, "Why?"

The reason I ask is to find out what is below the surface. Then I can deal with whatever *that* objection is.

24. My friends will think I am crazy if I accept Jesus.

Again I apply the "Why Principle": "Why will your friends think you are crazy?"

"They like to party and have fun. If I suddenly stop, they will think I've gone nuts."

"Yes," I say, "but let me ask you, if they are really your friends, won't they be happy and thrilled the God of the universe lives inside of you and all of your sins are forgiven?

"After all, when they see you change, they may want what you have."

25. The argument never stops.

This is the person who argues and argues and argues. When I run into somebody like this, my first reaction is to pray, "Lord, he is just like I used to be. Help me love him, Lord, until he understands the gospel."

Usually this type is filled with hostility. So I purposely avoid everything he wants to argue about. Instead, I have a tendency to ask questions like, "Why are you so angry? Why does the presentation of the gospel make you hostile?" Then I ask the key question: "If for some reason you found out everything I have said about the gospel and about Jesus is true, what would you do about it?"

If he tells me he will still not believe, I ask, "Why?" This may get me to his real objection, which I can deal with. But if in answer he says he is not ready or refuses to believe, I must remember it is OK to walk away from the presentation. But that does not mean I stop loving and praying for him. I watch for ways to speak to him someday in the future.

But if this person indicates he would be willing to believe if the gospel were true, I say, "That's wonderful, because I was the same way." Then I give him a short testimony of my life, how I argued and didn't believe who Jesus claimed he was. I like to give my testimony because Scripture reminds us in Revelation 12:11, "They overcame him by the blood of the Lamb, and by the word of their testimony."

People will come to Christ by the power of the gospel and our testimony.

Next, I look for a transition so I can open my Bible and show him the Scripture. I might say something like, "I was pretty open with you about my life. What was the most traumatic thing that has ever happened to you?" "Do you have a fear?" "Are you afraid of death?" "Did your parents ever hurt you?" "Would accepting God's love scare you to death?" "Has anyone ever loved you?" or "Do you ever feel alone?"

What I am trying to do is get below the surface of his defense mechanism. Once he is willing to talk about those subjects he has hidden from view in his arguing personality, I am well on the way to getting permission from him to share the gospel.

If he doesn't accept the gospel, don't let it drive you crazy. What is so obvious to you now, at one time was not so obvious. The Bible you hold dear, probably at one time, had no meaning to you. Worship services, probably at one time, were boring. Going to church and praying, probably at one time, seemed like a dull way to spend your life. This is because, as Scripture reminds us in 1 Corinthians 2:14, "The natural man receiveth not the things of the Spirit of God: for they are foolishness unto him: neither can he know them, because they are spiritually discerned."

Once, when I was active in prison ministry, I met a brilliant detective from Pueblo, Colorado, who had arrested many of the prisoners I knew. He had a reputation for cracking the toughest cases. And he had an argumentative attitude.

One day when he was at the jail, I went over and introduced myself to him. "Jack, I wonder if you would be willing to have lunch with me? I'd like to bring some of the ex-offenders you've arrested. Are you afraid?"

"No way."

"Good, then I'll bring my wife so you will know this is not a setup."

At lunch, Bruce, a six-foot-six ex-con with tattoos from his nose to his toes and an arrest record six and a half feet long with raps like murder and kidnapping, shared his testimony with Jack. Later, when Jack answered a page back to police headquarters, we could hear him say, "You won't believe who I'm having lunch with. I'm telling you, a God-thing is going on here. I've never seen anything like it in my life."

Though Jack did not accept Christ that day, I continue to share the gospel with him. I can see God is working, and I continue to pray for him on a daily basis. Whenever I begin to worry about him, I go out and find him again. I suppose I could quit out of frustration and stop loving and caring, but then I remember God did not quit on me.

So I pray, "Lord, until you say otherwise, I am going to look for every opportunity to take him to church, to lunch, and wait for an opportunity to see you change his life."

It may be frustrating, but I feel this is part of my sanctification process, so I am grateful for the frustration.

26. The church only wants my money.

I respond, "Has the church ever asked you for money? It's true that most churches take an offering. But it is usually the members who are expected to give, not the visitors.

"You see, God doesn't want to take your money. When you become a believer, something happens to your heart. You give because you want to. If you don't give in joy, you shouldn't give at all.

"The church doesn't want to take your money; the church wants you to surrender your life to Jesus. Are you willing to do that?"

27. There are many paths to God.

When I hear this objection, I nod. "You are correct; all roads lead to God. But here's the problem: what are you going to say when you get there? For God is either going to meet you as your Savior or as your judge. For Scripture says, 'That at the name of Jesus every knee should bow, of things in heaven, and things in earth, and things under the earth; And that every tongue should confess that Jesus Christ is Lord, to the glory of God the Father'" (Phil. 2:10–11).

28. There are many religions in the world.

Some people will say, "There are many religions in the world, and I don't know how a person can know the right one." I reply, "I've discovered that all of the religions in the world can be divided into two groups. Imagine, every religion other than Christianity is in my left hand—Mormonism, Buddhism, Hinduism, Judaism, whatever 'ism'—and Christianity is in my right hand. Everyone in my left hand makes two distinctive claims: (a) Jesus is not God, or he is not the only God. He may be a great prophet, teacher, or good man, but not the Messiah; and (b) If you do enough *good works*, such as good deeds, rid the world of infidels, or follow a special diet, you can receive some form of salvation.

"Two opposite claims cannot possibly be true. I would be willing to admit that if the 'ism' pile is true, my faith would be in vain. Would you be willing to admit, if the Christianity in my right hand is true, that your faith is in vain? Let's examine the evidence so we can find out which one of us is possibly in error.

"Christianity claims that Jesus is God, that God has come to us in Jesus who lived, died on the cross, and rose from the grave that we might have eternal life. Christianity claims, 'For by grace are ye saved through faith; and that not of yourselves: it is the gift of God: Not of works, lest any man should boast'" (Eph. 2:8–9).

I ask, "Can both of these teachings be true? All of us have to make a decision to place our trust in one view or the other." This turns a complicated argument into a simple answer.

29. There are many translations of the Bible.

In chapter 5, see "Too many translations" under "Objections to the Bible," or see response 29 in appendix 2.

30. There are many errors in the Bible.

In chapter 5, see "Too many errors" under "Objections to the Bible," or see response 30 in appendix 2.

31. There are too many hypocrites in the church.

To this objection I first say, "You are absolutely correct. There are hypocrites in every church. I'm so glad you are concerned about that, because when you join the perfect church, it won't be perfect any longer.

"Jesus said not to follow hypocrites but to follow him. I think it is exciting that you know the difference between a hypocrite and a genuine person. It will be fun to see you grow in your faith."

Then I add, "Trust me, if you accept Christ as your Savior and I see you begin to act like a hypocrite, I will remind you of this conversation. Are you ready to pray?"

One of Linda's friends, Jan, recently told her, "I am concerned by all the TV Christians who want you to send them money in exchange for prayer and miracles. If that's what Christianity is, I don't want any part of it."

Linda said, "Many TV Christians are genuine, but some are not. Think of it this way; if I falsely represented myself to you as a realtor in order to scam your money, does that mean all realtors are dishonest?"

"Of course not," Jan said.

"Then just because a person says he represents Christ, that does not mean he is a representative of Christ. Only Christ knows his heart."

Her friend nodded. "I hadn't thought of it that way before."

Linda asked, "Are you going to let a dishonest person stand in the way of knowing God's love for you?"

Linda reports that as of this writing, Jan is still processing the gospel, but she at least no longer has this roadblock in her way.

32. What about my family?

In chapter 3, see fear 5, "I'm afraid of losing my friends and relatives," or see response 32 in appendix 2.

33. What about those who never hear the gospel?

Linda had the opportunity to share the presentation with a longtime friend. He asked, "But what about those who never get a chance to hear the gospel?"

She said, "That's not you, is it?"

"No."

"Perhaps the question is, what does the Bible say will happen to those who have heard and have not responded?"

Stuart replied, "They will go to hell."

She said, "You've heard the gospel. Will you respond?"

He nodded. "Yes," he said, and Linda joyfully watched him receive Christ as his Savior.

34. Why does God let bad things happen?

This objection can appear to be difficult to deal with, but you must trust the Holy Spirit. I remember doing a seminar in which I was speaking to about six hundred teens. All during the seminar, I noticed the reaction of a teen who sat off to the side of the church. At break, I headed straight for her like a homing pigeon. I said, "Hi, what's your name?"

"My name is Patty."

"Are you a regular at this church?"

"No, I'm not."

"Have you found the Lord Jesus Christ yet."

She practically shouted, "No!"

I responded, "Why, Patty?"

In the next few minutes I became a part of a hysterical, painful reaction, the likes of which I have never experienced in all my years of ministry. Without taking a breath, Patty said, "What kind of God would allow my father to sexually abuse me from the time I was born to the time I was ten? What kind of God would let my stepfather take over from age ten to thirteen? What kind of God would let my minister violate me? What kind of God would let my only friends be burned alive in a terrible accident?"

I found myself backing up, physically as well as emotionally.

Then I thought of the example of Christ when he was confronted by the Pharisees with a difficult question. The Pharisees said, in John 8:4–5, "Master, this woman was taken in adultery, in the very act. Now Moses in the law commanded us, that such should be stoned: but what sayest thou?"

If Jesus said yes to stoning, he was condoning murder, and if he said no, he would break the Jewish law. These men thought they had trapped him at last. I learned much from Christ's response. First, he allowed the Pharisees to talk. When they finished, he turned the tables on them by asking them a question. In John 8:7 he said, "He that is without sin among you, let him first cast a stone at her."

In essence, Jesus asked, "What about you? Are you sinless?"

I took Jesus' response and applied it to Patty. I gently asked, "Patty, who taught you to tell your first lie?"

She looked at me through her tears and said, "No one had to teach me to lie."

"You are right, Patty. Remember the story about the garden of Adam and Eve? Before they disobeyed God, the garden was perfect. No one was molesting anyone. There was no evil because there was no sin. When Adam and Eve disobeyed God, sin entered the world and into us. Now we live in a fallen world, and we are fallen in the world. That is why no one had to teach you to lie. It is built into your nature. It's built into all of our natures to be self-serving and selfish. It's part of the Adamic curse. But this does not answer your toughest question. Why didn't God stop those men from hurting you? Why didn't God protect your friends from the fire? I can answer the question for you if you give me permission. But you won't like it."

"Go ahead."

"My answer is I don't know, but I do know this: you can walk through the rest of your life alone in your pain, or you can choose to hold onto a nail-scarred hand."

It was then that Patty knelt at the altar. After she prayed the sinner's prayer, she continued, "God, if you will forgive all of those men who violated me, I will make you a promise. I promise that one day I will forgive them also."

Wow! The beauty of Patty's prayer is that it was wrought through the power of the Holy Spirit. He is our power source. Through him, we can face this difficult question with an honest answer.

35. You can't possibly know what truth is.

It is a terrible tragedy that our culture has taught us to believe there are no absolutes, no right or wrong, and no truth. I have handled this objection in several ways. Sometimes, I merely ask, "Why?" and listen to someone flounder, trying to respond.

Yet, sometimes, with a gleam in my eye, I ask to borrow her watch. When she hands it to me, I put it into my pocket. Next, I talk about anything, except the fact that I have her watch in my pocket. In a while, she gets a little nervous and asks, "May I have my watch back?"

I say, "No, my truth is taking watches from people who don't believe in truth."

Finally, I reach in my pocket and pull out the watch and hand it back. I say, "You just told me there are no rights or wrongs. How can it be wrong if I steal your watch?"

When she can't answer me, I say, "See, you cannot hide behind that statement. May I show you some verses of Scripture that have had a major impact on my life?"

One day, I was standing in a restaurant when an old friend from my past said, "Hi, Bill. I thought I recognized you. I heard about all the changes in your life, and I wanted you to know that I'm spiritual too."

The word *spiritual* is a red flag to me; it usually means New Age.

I asked my friend if she had time for a cup of coffee. We sat down, and I asked, "Does truth matter to you?"

"You cannot know what truth is."

I looked across the table and said, "Then I am sure you'd have no problem whatsoever if I raped you."

She looked stunned. Her lower lip started to tremble.

I asked, "What's wrong?"

"Someone did that to me once."

I looked her right in the eye and asked, "Why was it wrong?"

Because of her horrible philosophy, she shook for five long minutes. She couldn't even tell me why the ultimate violation against a woman was wrong. Finally, I couldn't stand it any longer and said, "Let me tell you why it's wrong; it's wrong because God said so."

A few days later she called. "I've been thinking about what you said. Is it possible I could meet the God you are talking about?"

I'm happy to report she met the God of absolutes and truth. His name is Jesus Christ.

36. You must think you're better than me.

I like to say, "First of all, I am not better than anyone else; I am simply better off. Like everyone, I had broken God's commandments and laws and was condemned to hell. But by his grace and unfailing love, God sent someone into my life to tell me about Jesus. That made me realize how dirty I was in the presence of a holy God. I asked God to forgive me, and he did. It doesn't make me better than you; it makes me forgiven. Now I am giving you the same opportunity someone gave me."

Review

Let's review the way to handle an objection:

You: Are you ready to invite Jesus Christ into your life?

Friend: No.

You: Why?

Friend: I'm not ready.

You: Why?

The response your friend gives will better equip you to answer his objection. For a quick review of the preceding objections and their responses, see appendix 2.

Chapter 9

DEVELOPING AND KEEPING NON-CHRISTIAN FRIENDS

Why should you reach back into the world to share your faith with non-Christians? They are happy where they are and don't want to be bothered, right? True, the fallen world can appear disinterested in the good news. But don't let appearances fool you. There are many reasons why you should witness to others.

- **Christ died for them.**

Romans 5:8 tells us, "But God commendeth his love toward us, in that, while we were yet sinners, Christ died for us."

This is good news because at one time, we were fallen too. Not only did God love us anyway; he died for us, just as he died for our unsaved friends, family, coworkers, and acquaintances.

- **He loves them too.**

Luke 19:10 tells us, "For the Son of man is come to seek and to save that which was lost." This is yet another reason why we should reach back into the world. In Matthew 9:36–38 we can clearly see that the heart of Jesus was drawn toward the multitudes: "When he saw the multitudes, he was moved with compassion on them, because they fainted, and were scattered abroad, as sheep having no shepherd. Then saith he unto his disciples, The harvest truly is plenteous, but the labourers are few; Pray ye therefore the Lord of the harvest, that he will send forth labourers into his harvest."

- **They desperately need Christ.**

Jesus still loves the multitudes today. Their numbers may be greater, but their needs are the same. They need the Good Shepherd; they need his love, forgiveness, compassion, and help.

Many are drowning in hurting marriages, drugs, alcohol, loneliness, and lack of purpose. Their loneliness is a God-shaped vacuum that can be filled only with a relationship with God himself. Whether they are a person in a three-piece suit behind a mahogany desk, a businesswoman who looks so "together," a young mother, a teen, or a student—those without Christ are empty.

- **He called us to be "fishers of men."**

Were we not called to fish for men? Matthew 4:19 says, "And he saith unto them, Follow me, and I will make you fishers of men."

A "fisher of men" is someone who throws a lifeline to those thrashing in the sea of despair. In reality, the unbeliever is desperate to be rescued by the truth of God's love and salvation.

We Need to Make Non-Christian Friends

God calls us to go into his harvest. If you are living in isolation from the world and the only friends you have are in your comfortable Bible study, Wednesday night church get-togethers, Sunday school, Christian picnics, retreats, homeschool events, and concerts, you will never experience the joy of sharing your faith. Your life will become dry because you are ignoring the call to work in his fields. You will lose a sense of vitality that comes from obedience to the Great Commission.

God did not call you to hide from the world. He called you to go into the world. After all, the world cannot know Jesus if we keep his identity a secret. We must go and tell others who he is. Remember Romans 10:15, "How beautiful are the feet of them that preach the gospel of peace."

Matthew 28:19 reminds us to "go ye therefore, and teach all nations." We need to go because we cannot make disciples at a distance.

The message of Jesus' good news continues to ripple from one heart to the next. This ripple effect washed into our own lives and will continue to flow to others. If you are obedient, eternity will expand to include those people to whom God has called you to tell the good news.

There Is No Coincidence

God sends many people into my life. Some come only for a moment; others, for months or even years. Perhaps God will use me as a conduit to show them the good news of his Son. For this reason, I believe their presence in my life is by no means a coincidence.

Speaking of coincidence, I was teaching how to share Jesus without fear at a conference for a Christian legal society. Toward the end of the second day, a man named Larry Kelly came up to me and said, "All my doubts are gone."

I did not have a clue as to what he was talking about. "What do you mean, sir?"

"I'm ready."

"For what?"

"I want to give my life to Jesus."

I was surprised. After all, this was a conference for committed believers. I asked, "How did you get here?"

Larry told me his story. He said, "About a week ago, we were having a ferocious blizzard. My office was closed for the day, so I decided to clean out the basement so my son could have his own room.

"As I worked, I felt nagged about the existence of God. I took a load of books upstairs and one fell on the landing. When I picked it up, I was surprised to see it was a book about Jesus. I was surprised because I didn't even know I owned a book like that. Right then and there, I decided to read it from cover to cover.

"When I finished, I was even more confused. That's when I remembered there was a Christian bookstore not far from my house. So there I was, driving to the bookstore in the middle of a blizzard.

"When I arrived, Bruce, a salesman, was surprised to see me out on such a day. Since I was his only customer, we had time to chat. I asked him if he had any books on doubt. He didn't, but he began to tune into the fact that I was a struggling nonbeliever. When he found out I was a lawyer, he told me about this Christian legal conference that was to be held eighty miles from our town. That was a coincidence, because a client had already told me about it. Still, I almost didn't go, but my wife talked me into it at the last minute. So here I am."

Don't you love the way God works? Let's look at our list of so-called coincidences. First, as Larry began to wonder about God, the right book fell out of a stack of books. Then Larry's friends had told him about the conference as did the man at the bookstore. Larry came and found the Lord. By "coincidence," I happened to know and direct him to a Bible-believing church near where he lived. He's now in a men's Bible study with seventy other men. He continues to grow in his faith.

Never ignore the coincidence of the people God has placed before you. Instead, look for ways to build relationships, then you can use the "Share Jesus Presentation" to build a bridge.

Building Relationships

There are many ways to build relationships. We are limited only by our creativity and by our desire to please God.

- **Meeting Neighbors**

Unfortunately, today the sense of community is totally absent from many of our neighborhoods. Perhaps you could help change that in your community by taking a walk through your neighborhood to introduce yourself. You might want to contact your local police department to find out how to host a Neighborhood Watch program. When your neighbors meet in your home, if you feel led, perhaps even on a one-on-one basis, you can transition to the gospel by telling them that the thief comes to steal, but Jesus came to bring eternal life. You could also work with your local police department to sponsor a finger-printing and photograph party for the local kids.

- **Prayer Requests**

As you walk around your neighborhood, say to those you meet, "I am a person who prays a great deal, and I brought my notebook to write down prayer requests. Is there anything I could pray for?"

Later, when you are doing another walk-by, you may want to stop and ask, "I was curious, has that prayer been answered yet?"

If it has, your neighbor may be ready to answer your five "Share Jesus Questions." But regardless, you are still building a relationship.

- **Video Party**

Another idea is the next time you see both your neighbor and his wife out and about, say to the husband, "Hey there, John, I know you care a great deal about your marriage. We're going to have dessert and a video at my house next Tuesday night on how to improve our marriages. It's only going to last a half hour. Will you come?"

I dare the man to say no, especially in front of his wife.

- **Story Party**

You can also use the Tupperware approach to invite your neighbors to come and enjoy a festive time in celebration of spring, Valentine's Day, or whatever. The purpose of your celebration will be to allow everyone to sit around and share stories.

If it is around Christmas time, you might ask everyone to share his or her most important Christmas moment. Have a couple, who is perhaps not from the neighborhood, stand up for five minutes and share the real meaning of Christmas.

Pass out notecards and ask your guests to write their names and phone numbers. Next, say, "If anyone is interested in finding the real meaning of Christmas, put a little check mark on the card before you give it back to me."

You can also give them a pre-Christmas gift of a little envelope containing a gospel tract. You might suggest they read the last portion about how to have a relationship with Christ.

Later, if any of your neighbors check the card, call them back to ask if you can drop by to talk. Bring your sharing Bible/New Testament and "Share Jesus Questions" and present the gospel. If they respond, ask your neighbors if you can hold the next get-together at their places.

The reason you want to do this is because they will be able to invite different neighbors, family, and friends that you couldn't have reached. Like Tupperware parties, this Friendship Coffee can continue to travel to homes throughout your community. In one Texas town, 150 people were reached through a neighborhood outreach. They continue to meet in a recreation room and are currently looking for a pastor.

- **Special Interests**

We can build relationships through common interests, hobbies, sports activities, aerobics, quilting circles, and bowling leagues.

- **Kind Deeds**

A good deed is much like electricity: it may help someone see the light. One of my favorite ways to impact others is to shovel the snow off my neighbors' driveways. When they come home, tired from work, they cannot believe the driveway is done. With a little creativity, you can think of other ways to serve your family, friends, and neighbors.

- **Block Party**

In a large neighborhood, you can share your faith effectively by throwing a block party. It can be as economical as a dollar per person. This is an opportunity to get people involved in your neighborhood as well as at your church. Recently, several hundred people showed up for a barbecue block party sponsored by a church. Church members mingled with the crowd and shared the "Share Jesus without Fear Presentation." The church saw 238 people make decisions for Christ.

- **Community Service**

Perhaps you want to get your church involved in meeting the community. Perhaps your Sunday school class or youth group could go to a mall to wash car windows. You could leave a note saying, "We washed your windows because God loves you." Be sure to include the name of your church.

- **Old Friends**

If you have an old friend in your life with whom you have never shared the gospel and you are under conviction of the Holy Spirit, call your friend. Say, "I need to talk to you about something very personal. Let's set a time we can meet."

Pick a location where nothing disturbs you, no kids to distract, no husbands wondering where their dinner is. Just plan a private moment between two good friends.

Start off the conversation with an apology. "You know, I need to ask your forgiveness. I have not told you about the most important thing in my life. I have not shared how you could have a personal relationship with Jesus Christ, and I want you to know I'm so sorry."

Most of the time, your friend will try to help you recover by saying something like, "You don't have to be sorry—"

Say, "Yes, I do, because if you had died before we had this lunch today, I would know where you would be and I could never live with myself because I love you very much. I need and want to share with you how we can be together for eternity. I want to tell you how you can have a personal relationship with Jesus Christ."

Next, go into the five "Share Jesus Questions," then take your friend through the "Share Scriptures."

- **Reconnecting with People from the Past**

How can you go back to your past? Do you have relationships that have been marred, wounded, or insulted? The first principle you may need to recognize is the principle of waiting for God's timing.

I have learned a very simple way to recognize when God has decided it is time for me to write that letter or make that phone call or personal contact. I do this when a name from my past suddenly comes to mind.

People ask me, "Bill, wouldn't it be better if you waited and prayed about it first?"

I say, "I pray about it, but I don't wait because I'm wondering why that name did not come to my mind earlier."

I feel God brought it to my mind now, by the power of the Holy Spirit, because it is time to act. I immediately pray and I am ready to move.

It's like the time the Lord brought the name of Thomas, an attorney who once prosecuted me, to my mind. It had been ten years since our initial encounter, and I wondered what had happened to him. I prayed about it, then called him and asked if he'd be willing to go to lunch with me.

I knew because of the high-profile case, Thomas had kept track of me. I knew this would work to my advantage because my life had so radically changed.

I met with Thomas at lunch and shared what had happened in my life. I thanked him for being a part of God's plan to give me the jolt that would start me on my journey to find Jesus Christ.

In other words, I gave Thomas my testimony, and even though he did not respond, I had the privilege of planting a seed.

Several years later, Thomas's name came to my mind again, so I called him back and took him out to lunch. This time he brought a date, Meredith, his Christian girlfriend. I guess he either brought her to check me out or to enjoy the lunch because he knew she and I would have much in common. Once again, I reminded him of his need for the Savior. Still, nothing appeared to happen.

However, Meredith was going to a church where I would be speaking, and she invited Thomas to join us. A few weeks after he attended the presentation, I saw him again. To test the waters, I asked, "Do you have any spiritual beliefs yet?"

He kind of laughed and said, "You know what it is."

My heart jumped. "You have to tell me."

"I've given my heart to Jesus."

You could have heard me shout across the land.

So you see, God's timing was perfect. He can use the past to bond the future.

- **The Workplace**

A wise person once said, "A person's faith is not judged by what he says about it, but by what he does about it."

The people in your workplace are watching you, and I hope your integrity and work ethic would stand out like a shining star. Your coworkers will notice if you work hard, pick up after yourself and others, and don't waste company time or resources.

I often get asked in seminars about witnessing at work, and I am going to make a very surprising statement: I don't believe you should share at work, period. If your boss is paying you two dollars an hour, he does not want you to take his time to share your faith.

Coach Dave Nicholl says, "I always share on my own time. I try to honor God by being the best teacher and coach I can. My work ethic and commitment to others give me the opportunity to build relationships. When I share with students and their families, it is on my own time."

Dave has the right idea. You should not use company time to witness. Yet there is a difference between qualifying and sharing. You already learned to qualify a nonbeliever by simply asking the five "Share Jesus Questions." That takes only moments. You can qualify in a matter of seconds during a coffee break or in a hallway conversation.

When a coworker expresses an interest in knowing more, make an appointment to take him to dinner, lunch, Bible study, or church.

If you happen to be the boss, possibly in a management position, or if you run an office, such as a medical doctor's, you have to be extremely cautious because people will perceive you have a certain amount of authority over them.

You will want to take advantage of the Holy Spirit, not your authority. This means you will have to listen carefully to the clues your employees give you. A clue might be if someone confides something like: "Life is bad," "I don't know what to do," "I'm angry at my husband," "My teen drives me crazy," "I never seem to get well," or "My mother's dying." Also, you may pick up on body-language clues. Perhaps one of the employees is staring into space or seems upset, angry, or indifferent. These signs may be an opportunity for you to come alongside and say, "Are you OK?"

If the employee chooses to dump the truck and share his pain, be a great listener. There may be an opportunity, in a very gentle way, to say, "You know, I've had many problems as well, and I've found a solution to my pain."

If he asks about your solution, then you have permission to share. I would do it quickly and with discernment.

We will discuss sharing at work in more detail in chapter 11.

- **Be Nice**

It is so important to be nice to others. Take to heart Jesus' admonition, "Therefore all things whatsoever ye would that men should do to you, do ye even so to them" (Matt. 7:12).

In other words, look for ways to serve others, and by all means, hold that temper. If you should let it fly, don't be too proud to apologize. For when you reach out in love, others may see the light. Jesus said in Matthew 5:14–16, "Ye are the light of the world. A city that is set on an hill cannot be hid. Neither do men light a candle, and put it under a bushel, but on a candlestick; and it giveth light unto all that are in the house. Let your light so shine before men, that they may see your good works, and glorify your Father which is in heaven."

- **A Friend in Pain**

Often, people, out of desperation, loneliness, or limited acquaintances, are very willing to talk openly about their troubles. When this happens, the first thing we must do is to listen, because the principle behind listening is love. We are not only listening to what someone is saying, we are listening to what God is saying; we are listening to find the best way to love this person. When someone expresses a hurt, we must be careful we don't just peel off a Bible verse and give her a flip "I'll pray for you."

When we say, "I'll pray for you," we should also offer responses such as "That must have been terrible," "I'm so sorry," "Is there anything I can do?" or "What would you like me to do?"

Sometimes, a card shows an extra degree of thoughtfulness and could be left on the person's desk or sent to her home. It is another way of saying we are genuinely different because we put feet to our hearts.

Perhaps you just want to take a meal and drop it anonymously by her home; perhaps it is time to mow a yard, shovel a driveway, or send a gift certificate for dinner. All of these things can build a bonding relationship when a friend is most in need.

If you notice, I did not suggest you ask the five "Share Jesus Questions." This is a time to merely shine a light into the darkness. When you do, almost inevitably, your hurting friend will know who and what you are. You see, one of the most powerful evangelistic tools is love. I can almost guarantee you that at some time in the near future, God will create an opportunity for you to share your faith on a more personal level.

- **Other Ideas**

To share your faith at other times, invite someone to go shopping or share a meal or a coffee break.

Don't Be Afraid

Once, when I was teaching a seminar, I gave an assignment to the group to go out and ask the five "Share Jesus Questions." A woman came to me and gushed, "I'm going to ask my bowling team!"

When I saw her the next week, she said, "Bill, I've bowled with those women for five years. When I asked the questions you taught me, I was shocked to find out all five women were born-again and active in their church. Not once had we shared with one another."

Wow! To spend your life with others and to never know where they stand and for them to never know where you stand. We can't let this happen.

But you may say, "I'm afraid I will start to share with a friend, and she will close the door in my face. What will I do then?"

Closed Doors

When I share my faith with a friend and she rejects the gospel, my first reaction is to feel rejected and hurt. But I have to remind myself, it is Jesus she is rejecting—Scripture she is rejecting—not me.

I take a deep breath and say, "OK, Lord, I will wait for the moment you create."

But like a good fisherman, I don't quit fishing. If God has put someone on my heart, I may change my lure, I may go to a different fishing spot, and I may even try a different method of fishing.

All the while I will remind myself not to become so focused on the fish that got away that I miss other fishing opportunities. Besides, I have learned God may use this situation to intensify my prayer life as he teaches me to let go and wait.

Letting go may not go well with our hopes and dreams for our loved ones, but we must trust God. After all, he desires our loved ones to come into a relationship with Christ even more than we do.

For the past couple of decades, I have had people in my life who have been annoyingly uninterested in a relationship with Christ. That's OK. I'm waiting for God's perfect timing because someday in the future, they may be open to the gospel.

You see, at times in a relationship, I have been nose to nose with someone, sharing the gospel. At other times the gospel never crossed my lips.

My purpose in a friendship is not to ask the five "Share Questions" whenever we get together. My purpose is to be interested in a person's life and to let her know I love her.

We can't forget that we share our faith because we love others. Yet it is easy to be discouraged when the ones we love don't respond. A friend of mine was telling me about her pastor, who was discouraged. Every time he tried to share his faith, he got the answer, "No!"

If this should happen to you, let me remind you that God is pleased you were obedient. When a friend says no, whose problem is it, yours or God's? Could it be that God is sanctifying you so you will know how he feels when he is rejected by those he loves?

As you examine your own heart, don't look for a reason to quit. Instead, look to be obedient, just as Jesus did. Even though he had to face the cross, he never quit.

Perhaps you need permission to walk away from trying to force someone to accept the gospel. After all, you don't need to solicit a phony decision for Christ. Your only desire should be for a friend's genuine conversion, born out of the power of the Holy Spirit. You may even have to apologize to the one you tried to force salvation upon. Say, "I am so sorry I tried to make you become a Christian. I now realize the choice is yours, not mine. Please forgive me for trying to force this decision upon you."

Elaine, who was engaged to be married to Rick, said, "It wasn't until I apologized for trying to force my will on my fiancé, that he was finally able to consider the gospel. Before, the salvation message had been a battle of our wills, not a battle of his heart."

Remember, sometimes people don't respond to the cross. Even at the crucifixion, people cursed Jesus, stole his clothing, mocked him, spit at him, and tortured him, yet he remained faithful. That is our higher calling, to remain faithful. Of course, there is always the hope of a last-minute conversion, but that is not our motive. Ours is a walk of faith, not by sight, but to do all we can do to be obedient and trust God for the results.

Maintaining Relationships

How do we maintain relationships with friends who have not responded to the gospel? When people come into my life who know where I'm coming from, who are expecting me to share my faith at any moment, I have a great deal of fun. I just spend my time loving them. Almost always it bugs them. They will ask me, "Well, are you still doing churches? Are you still reading the Bible?"

I sometimes answer with a simple yes. In situations like this, I wait for the inevitable tragedy that will come into their lives. I know there will be such moments because no one gets through this world unscathed. When they come, I want to be there in expectancy and love.

Lifestyle Evangelism

This chapter has really been about lifestyle evangelism. To me, lifestyle evangelism is when we live our lives in a way that is open, vulnerable, caring, and matched by equal amounts of integrity and character. This way, people will be fascinated by our differences and motives. The undergirding this lifestyle brings is a deep love for people and a deep devotional life with God—because it is out of the overflow of our hearts that people will come to know him.

Jesus lived the perfect balance of lifestyle evangelism. He was willing to touch the untouchable, to love the unlovable, and to teach and correct the unteachable. Everything Jesus did was based on his love for his Father as well as his love for others, so always be ready to give the reason for the hope within you (1 Pet. 3:15).

Chapter 10
HOW TO PRAY FOR NONBELIEVERS

Our prayer lives are a measure of how well we are doing in other areas of our spiritual lives. For this reason alone, I encourage you to take time out of your busy day to pray. Your prayers should include praise and worship, confession of sins, and intercession for yourself and others.

As you pray, you become more aware of God's presence in your own life. As 1 Thessalonians 5:17 points out, we are to "pray without ceasing." This is great advice because if we have an ongoing conversation with God, we will always find ourselves seeking his presence. I like what Mother Teresa's business card said: "The fruit of silence is PRAYER. The fruit of prayer is FAITH. The fruit of faith is LOVE. The fruit of love is SERVICE. The fruit of service is PEACE."

Through prayer, we are led to faith, love, service, and peace. Jim Cymbala, a pastor from Brooklyn, New York, would agree. He tells his story in the book *Fresh Wind, Fresh Fire*. He relates that he came to a point at which unless God broke through, the ragtag Brooklyn Tabernacle he pastored was doomed to closure. Not only was his small church in trouble; he could not shake his winter cold that had dragged on for months. Finally, Cymbala's in-laws sent him to St. Petersburg, Florida, to get some much-needed rest for his congested lungs. One day, this young pastor was on a fishing boat with twenty tourists. He sat by himself and silently prayed, "Lord, I have no idea how to be a successful pastor. I haven't been trained. All I know is that Carol and I are working in the middle of New York City, with people dying on every side, overdosing from heroin, consumed by materialism, and all the rest. If the gospel is so powerful. . . ."

He couldn't finish because of his tears. It was then he sensed God speaking to him: *If you and your wife will lead my people to pray and call upon my name, you will never lack for something fresh to preach. I will supply all the money that's needed, both for the church and for your family, and you will never have a building large enough to contain the crowds I will send in response.*

When Pastor Cymbala got back to Brooklyn, he told his congregation, "If we call upon the Lord, he has promised in his Word to answer, to bring the unsaved to himself, to pour out his Spirit among us. If we don't call upon the Lord, he has promised nothing—nothing at all. It's as simple as that. No matter what I preach or what we claim to believe in our heads, the future will depend upon our times of prayer."[1]

Today, Pastor Cymbala has been the pastor of the Brooklyn Tabernacle for over twenty-five years. In that time, the congregation has grown from twenty members to more than six thousand. God has continued his work through this praying church.

Pastor Cymbala was right: ask nothing, get nothing. Jesus himself taught us, "Ask, and it shall be given you; seek, and ye shall find; knock, and it shall be opened unto you: For every one that asketh receiveth; and he that seeketh findeth; and to him that knocketh it shall be opened" (Matt. 7:7–8).

It's simple: if you don't ask, you don't get. We can enter into the heart of God only through prayer.

Pray before You Share

I cannot think of a single time, out of the thousands of times I have shared my faith, that I haven't prayed for the person beforehand. Even if it is a chance meeting, I silently pray for God's help.

Also, I have a list of unbelievers for whom I pray for daily. Some of these people have been on my prayer list for years; others, for only a short time. These people range from relatives to famous people God has put on my heart.

Kathie Grant understands the call to pray for unbelievers. She prays for twenty-five hundred unbelievers in a given week. Not long ago, she and her husband, Paul, were flying from Atlanta to Denver when she saw a senator who had been on her prayer list for seven years. He sat next to her, and she talked with him for three and a half hours. After a while, she asked, "Do you know what the gospel is?"

"No," he said.

There he was, sixty-six years old, and he had never heard the gospel.

Kathie asked, "Would you humor me and look at some verses from the Bible?"

"Sure," he said.

Kathie took him through the "Share Jesus Scriptures." Later, she said, "As he read the Scriptures aloud, I could see the Holy Spirit working."

He did not pray to receive Christ that day, but Kathie knows she was successful because she'd been obedient, not only to pray, but to share her faith. She says, "It was one of the highlights in my life."

I too have watched the power of prayer make a difference in an unbeliever's life. A few years ago, I took a major government official in law enforcement, a man whom I will call Ted, out to play golf. The group consisted of myself, Ted, and one other Christian named Zane. On the fifteenth hole, I turned to Ted and said, "Do you go to church anywhere?"

He rattled off five churches across the country. I asked, "If you died, where would you go?"

He strode two steps toward me and growled, "Fay, you know exactly where I'm going."

I wasn't about to back down, so I took two steps toward him. We were standing nose to nose, and I smiled and said, "Ted, I don't have a clue where you're going."

Out of the corner of my eye I saw my friend Zane literally bow and begin to pray. As he prayed, I could see Ted's heart melt. He said, "You're right, I don't know where I'm going either."

And right there, on the fifteenth hole of the Plum Creek Golf Course, he gave his heart to Christ. I am convinced I saw the power of intercession melt the heart of one who was resistant to God.

It is wise to pray for unbelievers. It is also wise to use prayer as a way to prepare you for sharing your faith. How can prayer help you get ready? For starters, you can pray for:

- **Opportunities**

Evangelism is a sanctification process. God is asking us to go into a deeper relationship with him. When I enter into prayer for the lost, I am asking God to open my eyes and my heart to the miraculous. Every morning, during my quiet time, I ask him to give me the privilege of sharing Jesus with somebody whose heart is ready to hear the good news. That way, I spend my day on alert, constantly asking, "Lord, is this the one you have sent to me today?"

This process makes me more open and available to move in God's will.

- **Love**

First Corinthians 13:1 says, "Though I speak with the tongues of men and of angels, and have not charity, I am become as sounding brass, or a tinkling cymbal."

It is hard to share our faith when our love for others has grown cold. For this reason, it is important to ask God to give us his love for others, to help us see their brokenness and pain, and to hear their cries. This kind of prayer will help us capture God's heart for the lost. Then we will share Christ, not out of duty, but out of love. Love makes all the difference.

Ephesians 3:17–19 says, "That Christ may dwell in your hearts by faith; that ye, being rooted and grounded in love, May be able to comprehend with all saints what is the breadth, and length, and depth, and height; And to know the love of Christ, which passeth knowledge, that ye might be filled with all the fulness of God."

When we begin to love others and look at them through God's eyes, we will see a people in darkness. In our country alone, according to the FBI:

- A murder occurs every twenty-one minutes.
- A rape occurs every five minutes.
- A robbery occurs every forty-six seconds.
- Aggravated assault occurs every twenty-nine seconds.

When we love others, the people trapped in the darkness are no longer statistics, but people Christ loves and died for. We know that their only hope is a born-again relationship with Jesus Christ. We pray they will find it.

- **Others Will See Christ in You**

Another constant prayer of our hearts should be that people will see Christ in us. We want God to use us as spiritual magnets to attract others to himself.

This will happen only when we are living in a prayer relationship with him. We will have the sparkle in our eyes that reveals the joy in our hearts. I pray that God will make your friends and family jealous enough of your joy to want it for themselves.

- **Boldness**

As the apostles did, we need to ask God for boldness. One day, after Christ's resurrection and ascension into heaven, the apostles were arrested for preaching the gospel in the temple. Before they were released from jail, they were threatened by the rulers of the synagogue. How did the apostles respond to those threats? They responded with prayer. They met in an upper room and prayed, "And now, Lord, behold their threatenings: and grant unto thy servants, that with all boldness they may speak thy word," At the end of their prayer, "the place was shaken where they were assembled together; and they were all filled with the Holy Ghost, and they spake the word of God with boldness" (Acts 4:29, 31). Their boldness came as an answer to prayer.

- **Power**

Pray that you know and recognize the power of God within you. Ephesians 1:18–19 says, "The eyes of your understanding being enlightened; that ye may know . . . what is the exceeding greatness of his power to us-ward who believe."

We need to be strong in the Lord and in his power. After all, we have the same resurrection power that raised Jesus from the dead inside of us! We lack absolutely nothing. Through prayer, we can "be strong in the Lord, and in the power of his might" (Eph. 6:10).

How to Pray for the Lost

Does God answer our prayers for the lost? Ask Big Earl. He had spent twenty-six years of his life in prison and had another twenty years to go. Two inmates, Tony and Don, witnessed to him one night. Big Earl's reaction was immediate. He gave Don a punch in the mouth, knocking out two teeth. Don got up, spit out his teeth, and said, "You can hit me again if you want, but I will never stop praying for you."

When Big Earl went into his cell that night, the Holy Spirit spoke to him, "Your sister has prayed for you for twenty-five years. It is now or never."

Big Earl said the voice was so clear he looked under his bunk and behind his toilet, wondering if someone had hidden a speaker in his cell. But as God's Holy Spirit penetrated his heart, Big Earl fell on his bed, convicted of his sins. When Tony and Don walked past his cell the next morning, they saw this big, six-foot-four man stand up and literally wring tears out of his pillow. God had moved on the behalf of the prayers of Big Earl's sister.

Psalm 2:8 says, "Ask of me, and I shall give thee the heathen for thine inheritance, and the uttermost parts of the earth for thy possession."

We pray for the salvation of others, not because we believe they are worthy of salvation, but because we believe in Christ's love, power, knowledge, and mercy. We pray because we know Christ desires all men to know him as Lord, just as he did us. We also pray to ask Jesus to send more workers into the field.

My prayer life was revolutionized after reading my friend Kathleen G. Grant's self-published book, *The Key to His Kingdom: Praying in the Word of God.* Kathie teaches the marvelous principle of praying God's will through his Word. She points to John 15:7, which says, "If ye abide in me, and my words abide in you, ye shall ask what ye will, and it shall be done unto you."

She explains prayer is a conversation with God, hearing him first through his Word, then responding back to him through his Word. She says, "To forego prayer is really like trying to do God's will without the breath of the Holy Spirit to energize and to bring the fruit. Nothing done apart from the Spirit will accomplish anything."

The following is a week's worth of Scriptures and prayers to help you pray for the lost. These prayers are from Kathie's book, *The Key to His Kingdom: Praying in the Word of God.*[2]

Directions: First, read the Scripture, then pray it back to God.

Day 1
Titus 3:5

"Not by works of righteousness which we have done, but according to his mercy he saved us."

Dear heavenly Father,

Just as you saved us because of your mercy, save our loved ones. Forgive us, we who already believe, for self-righteousness. We were once like the lost, and it was only your mercy, not our righteousness, that saved us.

Amen.

Day 2
1 Peter 3:18

"For Christ also hath once suffered for sins,
the just for the unjust, that he might bring us to God."

Dear heavenly Father,

Since Christ died for sins once for all, we ask that you apply his work to the following people so that they, like us, would be brought to you: *(names of people you want saved.)*

For the sake of Christ Jesus, who is worthy,

Amen.

Day 3
1 John 2:2

"And he is the propitiation for our sins: and not for our's only,
but also for the sins of the whole world."

Dear heavenly Father,

Since you have given Christ as an atoning sacrifice for the sins of the whole world, we apply his sacrifice to every nation on earth and pray that many within each may come to believe in him, just as we do. We know one thing: Jesus has already done it all! The payment he made is sufficient—may it now prove to be effective!

In his name,

Amen.

Day 4
Acts 2:21

"Whosoever shall call on the name of the Lord shall be saved."

Dear merciful Father,

How gracious you are that all sinners have to do is call on the name of your Son! That is because he has paid the price for everyone. Enable sinners to call! Send believers out to tell of his name—for how can they call on the one of whom they have never heard?

In the name of Jesus,

Amen.

Day 5
2 Corinthians 4:4

"In whom the god of this world hath blinded the minds of them which believe not, lest the light of the glorious gospel of Christ, who is the image of God, should shine unto them."

Dear heavenly Father,

Please have mercy on unbelievers just as you did on us before we believed. We too were at one time blinded by the devil. But in your mercy, you took the blindness from our minds so that we could believe in Christ and be saved. Do the same for unbelievers everywhere!

For the glory of your Son,

Amen.

Day 6
Colossians 4:3–6

"Withal praying also for us, that God would open unto us a door of utterance, to speak the mystery of Christ, for which I am also in bonds: That I may make it manifest, as I ought to speak. Walk in wisdom toward them that are without, redeeming the time. Let your speech be alway with grace, seasoned with salt, that ye may know how ye ought to answer every man."

Dear heavenly Father,

We do pray that you will open a door for us to tell the gospel to someone. We also pray for everyone else around the world who is doing the work of an evangelist, whether layperson, pastor, or missionary. Open up the door for the message of the gospel everywhere and in every nation. We pray that you will enable everyone who shares the message of Christ to proclaim it clearly as he should. We thank you for Bill Fay's *Share Jesus without Fear*, which is so clear and fulfills your will in this respect so wonderfully! May this method be brought to other Christians all over the world. Remind us, also, to be wise around unbelievers and to make the most of every opportunity. Make our conversations be full of grace and seasoned with salt.

According to the will of God,

Amen.

Day 7
John 16:24

"Hitherto have ye asked nothing in my name: ask, and ye shall receive, that your joy may be full."

Dear heavenly Father,

We ask in your Son's matchless name: answer our prayers for the salvation of the lost. Make our joy complete by giving Christ the largest inheritance possible!

In the name above all names,

Amen.

Kathie's book has many more Scriptures you can pray and rotate in your prayer journey, but these will help you get started. I also challenge you to pray over these and other meaningful Scriptures with your own prayers.

Prayer Lists

It may also help you to make a list of unbelievers for whom you can pray. And as Kathie says, "Dare to name anyone!" You may want to name friends, family, coworkers, politicians, government officials, movie and television personalities, doctors, nurses, secretaries, receptionists, sales clerks, hairdressers, neighbors, or in other words, anyone with whom you come in contact. If your list is very long, you may want to rotate it so you can cover everyone on your list in a week's time.

I have sat fascinated, studying Kathie Grant's personal prayer journal. Her journal lists the names of everyone from movie stars to bums on the street. I also found the date of when she started praying for the Berlin Wall to come down. But when I found my own name and the date she began to pray for me to become a Christian, I realized the awesomeness of her ministry. This was a giant reminder of the importance of intercession. Was the fact my name was in her prayer journal a coincidence? Let me put it this way: the more we pray, the more "coincidences" happen. In fact, God tells us in Philippians 4:6–7, "Be careful for nothing; but in every thing by prayer and supplication with thanksgiving let your requests be made known unto God. And the peace of God, which passeth all understanding, shall keep your hearts and minds through Christ Jesus."

I am so thankful that God answers prayers prayed on the behalf of unbelievers. I am living proof.

Chapter 11
LET'S GO

Someone once told a friend to be prepared for any opportunity. You never know when your preparation may save someone's life. This advice became clear to my friend one evening when he was dining in a restaurant. This is his story:

A man suddenly knocked a glass off the table and stood up, his face red and his eyes bulging. A piece of steak had lodged in his throat, and he couldn't breathe. I glanced around the room, hoping someone would rush to him to apply the Heimlich maneuver. But everyone froze, helpless. I pushed my chair back and ran to his side. When I wrapped my arms around his girth and squeezed, the meat dislodged from his throat, and I could hear the welcome sound of a deep breath.

Later, several people came by my table and expressed appreciation that I had helped. One gentleman said, "I'm so thankful you knew what to do. Could you tell me where I could learn to do that? I want to be prepared too."

The choking man's wife left a note for me with the cashier. It said, "Thank you. My husband wanted to thank you but was too

> embarrassed and weak to say anything. We are so thankful you weren't afraid to help us."
>
> But no one could have been more afraid than me. It wasn't absence of fear that made the difference; the difference was I was prepared. This experience taught me I might be the only hope for someone whose life hangs in the balance.

Just as knowing how to use the Heimlich maneuver can save someone's earthly life, knowing how to share Jesus without fear can help you save someone's eternal life. And you never know when you might be needed.

For example, an erroneous debit showed up on my checking statement. So I went down to the bank to see someone about it. A young woman, Krista, assisted me and took care of the problem. As I was about to leave, Krista said, "By the way, Bill, today is my last day at the bank."

"Really?" I asked. "I'm going to miss you. Not only because you fixed my problem, but because you're a kind person."

I could have dropped it there. It would have been easier to walk out the door, calling over my shoulder, "Have a nice life, Krista. Good luck!"

Instead, I decided to use the opportunity to share my faith, so I asked my favorite conversation-starting question. "Krista, I was wondering, do you go to church anywhere?"

"Well, I have been, once, with my friend."

"Has anyone ever told you the difference between religion and a relationship with Jesus Christ?"

"No. What *is* the difference?"

I said, "With your permission, I'll take you a step further."

So I sat at her desk and took out my sharing Bible/New Testament and let her read the Scriptures aloud. Then, as the Holy Spirit began to work, her tears began to fall. I asked, "Krista, are you ready to say yes to Jesus Christ?"

"Yes," she replied, and right there she did.

My question to you is, what if I had been reluctant to share with Krista? What if I had let this opportunity pass me by? What if I had been so focused on the bank's error, I had been rude and unloving toward Krista?

First and foremost, we must follow Christ's command to love our neighbors. We must talk to our neighbors with respect. Colossians 4:6 says, "Let your speech be alway with grace, seasoned with salt, that ye may know how ye ought to answer every man."

When we live our lives with a love-my-neighbor policy, we will take advantage of the opportunities God puts before us.

Ground-Breaking Obedience

Often, I hear my brothers and sisters say they want revival, a revival in which God moves and changes the hearts of individuals, families, communities, and nations. But I wonder: do we expect God to make the first move? If a farmer has broken no ground or sown no seeds, would he be justified in blaming God because he has no harvest?

Could we be like this lazy farmer? All of us should want revival, but revival will not come unless we break the sod of disobedience in our own hearts. Revival will not come unless we sow the seeds of the good news of Jesus Christ.

We have to respond. When was the last time you shared your faith or talked to someone with whom you didn't feel comfortable? When was the last time you wept and prayed for someone to come to Jesus Christ? When was the last time you sent a card to a family member who did not know the Lord?

On Judgment Day, it is not the liar, the murderer, the homosexual, or the fornicator who will stand before God in judgment first; it will be the household of faith. The person who rejected Christ will have to wait while we believers take our place in front. As they look on, we will have to look God in the eye and explain our every deed, done or undone; every word, spoken or unspoken (Matt. 12:36). Will we be embarrassed and ashamed because we have failed to obey the Great Commission: "Go ye therefore, and teach all nations, baptizing them in the name of the Father, and of the Son, and of the Holy Ghost" (Matt. 28:19)?

Will we grieve over the prayers we left unprayed, the sacrifices unmade, and the tears unshed? As we look behind us, into the faces of our condemned friends and family members, how will we feel?

I do not believe God is going to force obedience on us, because that is not his way. Love never forces anything. But when we disobey by choosing to ignore the Great Commission, God will allow us to experience spiritual dryness.

As I travel around to different churches, I have noticed that people's faith has grown weaker; their hearts, harder. Why? People are not experiencing God's joy because they are not sharing their faith. As we've studied, Philemon verse 6 says, "That the communication of thy faith may become effectual by the acknowledging of every good thing which is in you in Christ Jesus."

I believe God will discipline us so he can get our attention. I believe that if we do not go down on our knees, our nation will go down into oblivion. God will hold us responsible for the sin of silence for not sharing with those people he has placed in our lives.

The Time Is Now

Now that you realize you can't fail whenever you share your faith, you're ready to take the step of obedience. Don't be like so many who have approached me in tears. Many tell me they've felt God's gentle nudge to share with a friend and refused. One woman said, "I knew God was directing me to share with a friend who was in the hospital. But I was busy, and when I heard Lee was better, I ignored the nudge. 'There's plenty of time,' I thought. Two weeks later, Lee died unexpectedly."

She hung her head. "If only I hadn't waited."

People weep when they tell me these stories. They ask, "Do you think God will ever forgive me?"

They are feeling the shame of the sin of silence. They realize God wanted to use them as a messenger of the gospel, and they put it off. Now it's too late.

We don't know who's going to have tomorrow. We don't know if we're going to have tomorrow. The things we did yesterday are gone. What counts is to capture the moment God has given us today.

The only thing that counts is what we choose today—the moments we live for Jesus Christ. I never want to experience having to stand before God when he says, "Bill, why in the world were you ashamed to tell someone about my Son, Jesus Christ?" I'm going to stand before God for an awful lot of things, but I pray that's not one of them. I want to stand as the apostle Paul stood when he said in Romans 1:16, "For I am not ashamed of the gospel of Christ: for it is the power of God unto salvation to every one that believeth; to the Jew first, and also to the Greek."

Are You Burdened?

Christians have a misunderstanding. People often tell me they have an incredible burden for a friend or a relative or someone else. What I try to get them to understand is, when God gives you a leading, it's not the time to just go home and pray about it. It's the time to respond, immediately. God has been preparing this moment before the world began.

If he wanted you to wait, he'd have given you the idea tomorrow. If he wanted you to do it yesterday, the idea would have come the day before. But when he puts Susan or John on your mind, the timing is now.

Lee Strobel says in *Inside the Mind of Unchurched Harry and Mary*, "Almost every day, we come to evangelistic turning points. We make choices whether to help rescue these people from danger or to walk the other way. We make spur-of-the-moment decisions whether to heroically venture into their lives and lead them to a place of spiritual safety, or to merely hope that someone else will do it. . . . We make split-second decisions all the time to either play it safe or to tilt the conversation towards spiritual topics, and many times we shrink back."[1]

We must not shrink back. We must venture into the spiritual lives of others, to point the way to Christ.

Be Obedient to Your High Calling

Again, your responsibility isn't to cause a conversion. It is to be obedient to the high calling of the Great Commission.

Remember, success is sharing your faith, living your life out for Christ. It is not leading someone to Christ. Besides, as someone once said, "God never calls us to be successful, he calls us to be faithful."

If you choose obedience in sharing your faith, your Christian life will never dull because Philemon verse 6 will have been activated.

Evangelism is not just about the person with whom you are sharing, because even if you refuse, God can make the rocks cry out. Evangelism is about experiencing God. If you choose to be obedient, he will take you on a journey so exciting that your life will never be the same.

I have had the privilege to share my faith on a one-on-one basis twenty-five thousand times since I met the Lord in 1981. It is with absolute confidence I can say I have never led one person to Jesus Christ. But I stay excited as I see how the Holy Spirit continues to change the lives of those with whom I've shared.

Remember, earlier in the book, I said there are only two kinds of Christians in this world:

1. Those who talk *about* the lost.
2. Those who talk *to* the lost.

It is time to choose obedience and grasp the fullness of a Christian life. It is time to be the kind of Christian who will talk *to* the lost, who will die to himself, and who is never ashamed of the gospel. It is time to be the kind of Christian who is really making a difference. You can begin by asking someone one of the five "Share Jesus Questions" today. But more than just asking questions, you will have chosen obedience. And when people choose obedience, they experience a unique kind of joy in an ever deepening relationship with their Lord and Savior Jesus Christ. It is time to share Jesus without fear. God wants you to experience his joy. So get ready. It is time to *go!*

Appendix 1
SHARE JESUS REVIEW

Optional Conversation Joggers

1. May I ask you a question?
2. What are the biggest problems women face today?
3. What's your favorite sport? How much money would it take for a man's life to be perfect?
4. Do you go to church anywhere?
5. May I give you a five-question survey?
6. You know about my spiritual beliefs, but I don't know about yours. What are they?
7. Do you ever feel uncertain about what you are depending on spiritually for hope in your life?
8. Has anyone ever told you the difference between religion and a relationship with Jesus Christ?
9. May I have your permission to share seven Scriptures that changed my life?

10. How many people would it take flipping a quarter before one person hits heads thirty times in a row? *(billions)* One reason I believe the Bible is true is because of the thirty recorded prophecies of the birth, the death, and the resurrection of Jesus that have come true. That's a lot like landing heads thirty times in a row.
11. Does truth matter to you?
12. Has anyone ever explained Christianity to you?
13. I need to ask your forgiveness. I have not told you about the most important thing in my life. I have not shared how you can have a personal relationship with Jesus Christ, and I want you to know I'm so sorry.
14. You know, I've had many problems as well, but I've found a solution for my pain.

The Five Share Jesus Questions

These questions act as a funnel. You can start anywhere on the list, as you feel led, or skip straight to the "Share Jesus Scriptures."

1. Do you have any kind of spiritual belief?
2. To you, who is Jesus?
3. Do you think there is a heaven or a hell?
4. If you died tonight, where would you go? If heaven, why?
5. By the way, if what you were believing is not true, would you want to know?

Note: You might ask at this point: "May I share some Scriptures with you?" If the answer is yes, open your Bible to the next phase. If the answer is no, do nothing. But remember you have not failed. You have been obedient to share the gospel, and the results belong to God.

The Share Jesus Scriptures

Note: Ask your friend to read the verse aloud. Next, ask him, "What does this say to you?" If your friend gives an incorrect answer, say, "Read it again." Continue this process, until your friend understands the Scripture.

1. John 3:16—"God loves you."

"For God so loved the world, that he gave his only begotten Son, that whosoever believeth in him should not perish, but have everlasting life."

What does this say to you?

2. Romans 3:23—"All are sinners."

"For all have sinned, and come short of the glory of God."

What does this say to you?

3. Romans 6:23—"For the wages of sin is death."

"For the wages of sin is death; but the gift of God is eternal life through Jesus Christ our Lord."

What does this say to you?

4. 1 Corinthians 15:3–4—"Christ died and rose for our sins."

"For I delivered unto you first of all that which I also received, how that Christ died for our sins according to the scriptures; And that he was buried, and that he rose again the third day according to the scriptures."

What does this say to you?

5. John 1:12—"God's remedy for sin."

"But as many as received him, to them gave he power to become the sons of God, even to them that believe on his name."

What does this say to you?

6. Revelation 3:20a—"All may be saved now."

"Behold, I stand at the door, and knock: if any man hear my voice, and open the door, I will come in to him."

What does this say to you?

The Five Commitment Questions

1. Are you a sinner?
2. Do you want forgiveness of sins?
3. Do you believe Jesus Christ died on the cross for you and rose again?
4. Are you willing to surrender your life to Jesus Christ?
5. Are you ready to invite Jesus Christ into your life and into your heart?

Sinner's Prayer

Confessing to God that I am a sinner, and believing that the Lord Jesus Christ died for my sins on the cross and was raised for my justification, I do now receive and confess Him as my personal Saviour.

The Why Principle

You: Are you ready to invite Jesus Christ into your life?

Friend: No.

You Why?

Friend: I'm not ready.

You: Why?

New Believer Questions and Directions

1. How many sins has Christ paid for?
2. How many of your sins does Christ remember?
3. Where does Christ live?
4. Let's pray. *(New believer should say what's on his heart.)*
5. Who has been praying for you?
6. Do you know where your friend goes to church?
7. Do you know your friend's phone number? Let's call that person now!
8. May I take you to church with me?
9. Read the Gospel of John.
10. I will call you tomorrow to see if the Word became different.

Note: A quick reference to the objections and responses are listed in appendix 2.

Appendix 2

36 RESPONSE SCRIPTS TO OBJECTIONS

This alphabetical list of objections corresponds with the responses in this appendix as well as the responses listed in chapter 8.

Objection Topic List

How to Use This Section:

Let's say you are interested in finding the response to the objection, "What about my family?"

Look for "What about my family?" in the topic list above. There you will find, "What about my family?" can be found in this appendix three ways:

1. In alphabetical order.
2. On page 176.
3. Listed as objection 32.

Note: If you also want to reference the fleshed-out illustrations and stories of "What about my family?" turn to chapter 8. There you will also find this objection/response listed as objection 32 and placed in alphabetical order.

Responses to Objections:

1. A Christian hurt me.

You:

- I'm so sorry that happened. Would you accept my apology, for those who did that to you?
- *(If appropriate:)* Have you ever tried to love somebody and made a mess out of it? You had good intentions, but everything went wrong. Do you think there was a possibility in your friend's desire for you to know Jesus that she just went about it the wrong way?
- Jesus would not approve of rude behavior either. By the way, what is your understanding of who Jesus is?

2. Cults are the answer?

You:

- If what you believe is not true, would you want to know?
- Who is Jesus Christ? Isn't it interesting he said he was God? *(Read the following Scriptures aloud.)*

Read: "I and my Father are one" (John 10:30).

You: The literal translation of this means Jesus and the Father are of the same essence.

Read:

- "If ye had known me, ye should have known my Father also: and from henceforth ye know him, and have seen him" (John 14:7).
- "I am Alpha and Omega, the beginning and the ending, saith the Lord, which is, and which was, and which is to come, the Almighty" (Rev. 1:8).

You: We know this was Jesus speaking in Revelation 1:8 for the book closes with:

Read: "He which testifieth these things saith, Surely I come quickly. Amen. Even so, come, Lord Jesus" (Rev. 22:20).

Read:

- "Who is the image of the invisible God, the first-born of every creature: For by him were all things created, that are in heaven, and that are in earth, visible and invisible, whether they be thrones, or dominions, or principalities, or powers: all things were created by him, and for him" (Col. 1:15–16).
- "Before Abraham was, I am" (John 8:58).
- "God said unto Moses, I AM THAT I AM: and he said, Thus shalt thou say unto the children of Israel, I AM hath sent me unto you" (Exod 3:14).

You: The Jewish people wanted to stone Jesus because they knew he was referring to himself as God when he called himself, "I AM!" He was using the divine name of God found in Exodus 3:14.

Read:

- "Therefore the Jews sought the more to kill him, because he not only had broken the sabbath, but said also that God was his Father, making himself equal with God" (John 5:18).

- "Thomas answered and said unto him, My Lord and my God. Jesus saith unto him, Thomas, because thou hast seen me, thou hast believed: blessed are they that have not seen, and yet have believed" (John 20:28–29).
- "And again, when he bringeth in the firstbegotten into the world, he saith, And let all the angels of God worship him" (Heb. 1:6).

You: Did Jesus ever sin?

Read: "For we have not an high priest which cannot be touched with the feeling of our infirmities; but was in all points tempted like as we are, yet without sin" (Heb. 4:15).

You: Who can forgive sins but God alone? If Jesus were not God, how could he forgive sins and not sin himself?

Read: "And, behold, they brought to him a man sick of the palsy, lying on a bed: and Jesus seeing their faith said unto the sick of the palsy; Son, be of good cheer; thy sins be forgiven thee. . . . But that ye may know that the Son of man hath power on earth to forgive sins, (then saith he to the sick of the palsy,) Arise, take up thy bed, and go unto thine house" (Matt. 9:2, 6).

You: Why did Jesus allow others to worship him if he is not God?

Read: "And he said, Lord, I believe. And he worshipped him" (John 9:38).

You: May I show you a few Scriptures that changed my life? *(show the "Share Jesus Scriptures") or* May I tell you how Christ changed my life?

Note: Some will misunderstand that God the Son and God the Father are one in the same. If this happens:

You: I am a son and a brother *(or whatever pronouns best describe you)*. Although I have the different roles of being both a son and a brother, I am the same person. God is both God the Son and God the Father. He has different roles, but he is the same person. Would you like to know him?

Additional comments: Jesus said he was God. If he was a good man and never sinned, then how could he lie? He also allowed others to worship him and he forgave sins. How could he do this if he were not God?

Also see the objection/responses "I am a member of another world religion," "There are many religions in the world," and "There are many paths to God" in this appendix or chapter 8.

3. God cannot forgive me.

Read: "For whosoever shall call upon the name of the Lord shall be saved" (Rom. 10:13).

You:
- What does this say to you?
- Can God forgive a repentant murderer?
- Can he forgive a bank robber?
- Can God forgive you?
- *(If your friend answers yes)* Let's pray.

Additional comments: Also see the objection/response "I'm not good enough."

4. How can a loving God send someone to hell?

You: Why would God allow his Son Jesus to die on the cross for us if his death had no meaning?

Read:
- "He that spared not his own Son, but delivered him up for us all" (Rom. 8:32).

- "For the wages of sin is death; but the gift of God is eternal life through Jesus Christ our Lord" (Rom. 6:23).

You: Jesus died for us so we would not have to go to hell.

Read: "But God commendeth his love toward us, in that, while we were yet sinners, Christ died for us. Much more then, being now justified by his blood, we shall be saved from wrath through him" (Rom. 5:8–9).

You:

- If you reject Christ and his gift, what does Scripture say will happen to you?
- Jesus Christ never committed a sin in thought, word, or deed. Yet, on the cross, Jesus became our sin bearer. God turned his back on him and heaped all of his waves of wrath upon his own Son. This is a picture of God's perfect justice. Even one sin separates us from God, no exception. This is why Jesus died in our place. If this were not the case, don't you think that God would have spared his own Son? He died in your place. Would you like to be forgiven through his sacrifice?

5. How can I know the Bible is true?

You:

- How many people would it take flipping a quarter before one person hits heads thirty times in a row? (a billion)
- One reason I believe the Bible is true is because of the thirty recorded prophecies of the birth, the death, and the resurrection of Jesus that have come true. That's a lot like landing heads thirty times in a row.

- How many people would it take flipping a quarter before one person hit heads 245 times in a row? I picked that number because it is a conservative estimate of the number of biblical prophecies that have come true.

Read: "For the prophecy came not in old time by the will of man: but holy men of God spake as they were moved by the Holy Ghost" (2 Pet. 1:21).

You: May I share some Scriptures that changed my life?

Additional comment: See objection/response "There are many translations of the Bible" in this appendix or in chapter 8.

6. How do I know I have enough faith?

You:

- If you have enough faith to ask Christ to come into your heart, you have enough faith to receive him into your heart.
- Imagine Moses. As he led his people out of Egypt, he met a pretty big roadblock—the Red Sea. As Pharaoh's army closed in on Moses and the tribes of Israel, God directed Moses to cross the sea. Moses stood on the shore, wondering if he had enough faith. It wasn't until he put his foot in the water that the sea parted. God will honor your first step. If you really want to know Jesus as Lord, take the first step and ask him into your heart. Are you ready?

Additional comment: See objection/responses "I'm not sure I'm saved" and "I've tried it and it didn't work out" in this appendix or in chapter 8.

7. I can't live the Christian lifestyle.

You: I am glad you understand some change is required. But unlike the past, you are not going to have to change alone.

Read: "I can do all things through Christ which strengtheneth me" (Phil. 4:13).

You: God wants your "want to," not your ability. He wants your desire. Are you desiring now to follow Jesus Christ as your Lord?

Additional comment: If your friend says yes, it is time for the sinner's prayer.

8. I don't believe in God.

You:

- *(If this objection is stated at the beginning of the presentation, ask, Why?)*
- May I show you some Scriptures that changed my life? *(Show the "Share Jesus Scriptures.")*
- *(If this objection is stated at the end of the presentation, ask, Why?)*
- If you became convinced that God existed, would you be willing to give your life to him? Would you be willing to ask a nonexistent God to help you in your unbelief?

Pray: God, if you are real, help me to believe.

You: Let's talk again in a few days/weeks.

Additional comment: If further help is needed, recommend your friend read *More Than a Carpenter* by Josh McDowell.

9. I don't believe the Resurrection took place.

You: I'm glad this is your only stumbling block because one thing God did for us is provide overwhelming evidence of the Resurrection. In fact, a mock trial was held at Harvard University, and the conclusion was clear: the evidence overwhelmingly proved the resurrection of Jesus Christ.

Read: "And ye shall seek me, and find me, when ye shall search for me with all your heart" (Jer. 29:13).

You: If you want to test your heart right now, why don't you bow your head now?

Pray: Lord Jesus, if the Resurrection took place, help me in my unbelief.

Note: If your friend is ready, you may have him pray.

Pray: I am a sinner, I want forgiveness of all my sins. I want to believe that Jesus died on the cross for my sin.

You: Did you mean this prayer? For God will help you believe.

Additional comment: If your friend wants to see Scripture that talks about the deity of Christ, see objection/response "Cults are the answer?" Other objection/responses that may help are "I am a member of another world religion," "There are many religions in the world," "I'm Jewish," and "There are many paths to God."

10. I want to think about it.

Read: "For the wages of sin is death; but the gift of God is eternal life through Jesus Christ our Lord" (Rom. 6:23).

You:
- According to this, when you die, where are you going?

- Drive carefully. *(or)* Have a nice day.
- *(If your friend answers, "Hell," with fear and trembling)* Are you ready to accept Jesus Christ as your Savior?

Additional comment: If he says he is not ready, you will need to release him from this conversation, but be sure to give him your phone number if he wants to call you back in a few days. Keep praying. Also see objection/response "I'm not ready" in this appendix or chapter 8.

11. I'm a good person.

You:

- By whose standards?
- Have you ever committed murder?

Note: After your friend's response to the above question, do not allow time for him to respond to the following questions.

You:

- Let's check it out by God's definition. Have you ever been angry, hated, called someone a fool, or waved them off on the freeway? Because if you have, by God's standards you are a murderer.
- Have you ever looked at the opposite sex and lusted?
- By the way, if you say no, I know you are guilty of lying. But if you have lusted, by God's standards you are guilty of adultery.
- Have you put a relationship, a job, or some activity that you would rather do or have over a relationship with God? Because if you have, those items have become your idols.
- Because of the holiness of God, it is impossible to measure up to his standards of perfection. Since

God is the judge and the jury, it is his approval we have to meet.

Read: "For whosoever shall keep the whole law, and yet offend in one point, he is guilty of all" (James 2:10).

You: I want you to know that I, like you, have been guilty as well. The difference is I found forgiveness through Jesus. Do you want this kind of forgiveness?

Additional comment: Remember to be loving to your friend. God is still in control of his life. See objection/response "I'm not a sinner" in this appendix or chapter 8.

12. I'm a member of another world religion.

You:

- Has anyone ever told you about Christianity?
- Who taught you your first lie?
- Almost everyone has lied. No one had to teach me to lie. My parents or friends did not give me lying lessons. It came out of myself. It comes from our sinful nature.
- Let me tell you the story about Adam and Eve in the garden of Eden. Before they disobeyed God, the garden was perfect. There was no evil because there was no sin. When Adam and Eve disobeyed God by eating the fruit God forbade them to eat, sin entered the world and into us. That is why no one has to be taught to lie, cheat, steal, or lust, or to be envious of other people. It is part of the nature that is in us.
- Let me show you some Scriptures that help explain this idea. (*Show the "Share Jesus Scriptures."*)

Additional comment: See objection/responses "Cults are the answer?" "There are many religions in the world," "I'm Jewish," and "There are many paths to God" in this appendix or chapter 8.

13. I'm God.

You: I could use a new car; could you create one for me? Surely, an all-powerful God such as you could do that.

Read: "Thou shalt have no other gods before me" (Exod 20:3).

You: What does this say to you?

Read: "Who changed the truth of God into a lie, and worshipped and served the creature more than the Creator, who is blessed for ever. Amen" (Rom. 1:25).

You: What does this say to you?

Read: "Who hath delivered us from the power of darkness, and hath translated us into the kingdom of his dear Son: In whom we have redemption through his blood, even the forgiveness of sins: Who is the image of the invisible God, the firstborn of every creature: For by him were all things created, that are in heaven, and that are in earth, visible and invisible, whether they be thrones, or dominions, or principalities, or powers: all things were created by him, and for him: And he is before all things, and by him all things consist" (Col. 1:13–17).

You:
- What does this say to you?
- According to this Scripture, God is God alone. He is not "all things," but he is the Creator who holds all things together.

- I am not God, but he is in me. Would you like God to be in you?

14. I'm having too much fun.

You:
- Why?
- *(Echo back what your friend answers. Example:)* In other words, you are into the party scene—sex, drugs, and rock and roll.
- According to this, when you die, where are you going?
- Drive carefully. *(or)* Have a nice day.
- *(If he answers, "hell," with fear and trembling)* Are you ready to accept Jesus Christ as your Savior?

Additional comment: You may need to release your friend from this conversation, but be sure to give him your phone number if he wants to call you back in a few days. Keep praying.

15. I'm Jewish.

Note: When someone says he doesn't believe in Jesus, I ask, "Why not?" If he says he is Jewish,

You:
- Do you go to synagogue anywhere?
- Did you know that Judaism is the root of my faith in Christianity?
- I believe Jesus is the Christ, the Messiah. Did you know he claimed to be God?

Read: "I and my Father are one" (John 10:30).

You:
- I know he is not a liar, because he never sinned. He's obviously not a lunatic, because his life and

teachings show he was brilliant, stable, and loving toward others. Therefore, I can only believe he is Lord.

- Also, the Jews of the day clearly knew who Jesus claimed to be because they tried to kill him when he said:

Read: "Before Abraham was, I am." (John 8:58).

You: The Jewish people knew he was referring to himself with the divine name of God found in Exodus 3:14.

Read: "God said unto Moses, I AM THAT I AM: and he said, Thus shalt thou say unto the children of Israel, I AM hath sent me unto you" (Exod 3:14).

You: If either point, the point that Jesus is the Messiah or that he rose from the dead, were true, would you consider having a personal relationship with him to complete your Jewishness?

Additional comment: At this point, you may want to invite your friend to visit a Messianic congregation with you where he can see Jewish people expressing their faith in Christ. You may also want to give him a copy of Josh McDowell's book *More Than a Carpenter* or a copy of the Gospel of John to read. See objection/responses "I'm a member of another world religion," "There are many religions in the world," "How can I know the Bible is true?" and "Cults are the answer?" in this appendix or chapter 8.

You: (If I am talking to a practicing Jew, I continue.) "Have you ever wondered about the fact that Jesus claimed to be God?"

Read: Who hath believed our report? and to whom is the arm of the LORD revealed? For he shall grow up before him as a tender plant, and as a root out of a dry ground: he hath no form nor comeliness; and when we shall see him, there is no beauty that we should desire him. He is despised and rejected of men; a man of sorrows, and acquainted with grief: and we hid as it were our faces from him; he was despised, and we esteemed him not. Surely he hath borne our griefs, and carried our sorrows: yet we did esteem him stricken, smitten of God, and afflicted. But he was wounded for our transgressions, he was bruised for our iniquities: the chastisement of our peace was upon him; and with his stripes we are healed. All we like sheep have gone astray; we have turned every one to his own way; and the LORD hath laid on him the iniquity of us all. He was oppressed, and he was afflicted, yet he opened not his mouth: he is brought as a lamb to the slaughter, and as a sheep before her shearers is dumb, so he openeth not his mouth. He was taken from prison and from judgment: and who shall declare his generation? for he was cut off out of the land of the living: for the transgression of my people was he stricken. And he made his grave with the wicked, and with the rich in his death; because he had done no violence, neither was any deceit in his mouth. Yet it pleased the LORD to bruise him; he hath put him to grief: when thou shalt make his soul an offering for sin, he shall see his seed, he shall prolong his days, and the pleasure of the LORD shall prosper in his hand. He shall see of the travail of his soul, and shall be satisfied: by his knowledge shall my righteous servant justify many; for he shall bear their iniquities. Therefore will I divide him a portion with the great, and he shall divide the spoil with the strong; because he hath poured out his soul unto death: and he was numbered with the transgressors; and he bare the sin of many, and made intercession for the transgressors. (Isa. 53:1–12)

You:

- Who do you think this describes?
- Why do you think many synagogues refuse to read this chapter of Isaiah?
- Do you know why the sacrifices have stopped in the temple?
- *(Wait until they answer then ask:)* Could it be because Jesus is God's sacrificial lamb?

Additional comment: I don't push. My goal is to just have a warm, friendly discussion which will lead to other discussions. If he indicates an interest in learning more, I invite him to meet with a local Messianic pastor—who is far more of an expert on the Old Testament than I. A fellow Jew will be very sensitive to my friend's culture and feelings.

If I determine my friend does not attend synagogue and is what I call a "secular" Jew, then I take him through the same Scriptures about Christ found in my response to objection 2, "Cults are the answer?"

16. I'm not a sinner.

Read: "Jesus said unto him, Thou shalt love the Lord thy God with all thy heart, and with all thy soul, and with all thy mind" (Matt. 22:37).

You:

- Have you ever loved God with all your heart, soul, mind, and strength? No? That's what sin is.
- Let's turn to the next Scripture.

17. I'm not good enough

You:

- Why?
- That's one thing we have in common. We are not good enough. This is a problem. There are only two ways to get to heaven: either we have to be perfect, never once committing a sin in word, deed, or

thought, or we have to become born again. I can become born again by accepting in my heart the finished work and person of Jesus Christ who paid the penalty for my sins. He has the power to forgive me because of his birth, death, and resurrection. When I believe on him, and accept his forgiveness, only then can he erase the sins I have committed in the past. Personally, I opt to choose his forgiveness, because I can never be good enough to obtain perfection.

Read:

- "For by grace are ye saved through faith; and that not of yourselves: it is the gift of God: Not of works, lest any man should boast" (Eph. 2:8–9).
- "That if thou shalt confess with thy mouth the Lord Jesus, and shalt believe in thine heart that God hath raised him from the dead, thou shalt be saved. For with the heart man believeth unto righteousness; and with the mouth confession is made unto salvation" (Rom. 10:9–10).
- "For whosoever shall call upon the name of the Lord shall be saved" (Rom. 10:13).

You: Does this include you? Are you ready for God to forgive your sins?

Additional comments: See objection/response "God cannot forgive me" in this appendix or chapter 8.

18. I'm not ready.

You:

- Why? *(Allow your friend to answer.)*
- Are you really going to let *(his answer)* stand between you and God?
- *(If the answer is no,)* Are you ready to invite Christ into your life?

Additional comment: In response to your "Why not?" your friend may say, "I am not ready because this information is so new to me. This is a whole new way of thinking, and I want to count the cost." Be prepared to stop the presentation and to release your friend to God's sovereignty and control. Say something like, "I enjoyed our time and I will be praying for you. May I talk to you again in a few days or weeks?"

See objection/response "I have to think about it" in this appendix or chapter 8.

19. I'm not sure I'm saved.

Note: Sometimes you will meet someone who has genuinely asked Christ in his heart, but feels he is not saved.

You:
- That's a very nice watch. If you lost it, you'd miss it when you wanted to see the time. But if you've never owned a watch, you wouldn't worry about looking at it, nor would you worry about losing it.
- Don't you find it interesting that you are worried you are not saved? You can't worry about losing something you don't have. I bet before you asked Christ into your life, you didn't go around worrying that Christ was not in your heart.
- It is a wonderful confirmation to me that you might be saved because you are concerned.

Read: "For I am persuaded, that neither death, nor life, nor angels, nor principalities, nor powers, nor things present, nor things to come, Nor height, nor depth, nor any other creature, shall be able to separate us from the love of God, which is in Christ Jesus our Lord" (Rom. 8:38–39).

You: What does this say to you?

Read: "In whom ye also trusted, after that ye heard the word of truth, the gospel of your salvation: in whom also after that ye believed, ye were sealed with that holy Spirit of promise, Which is the earnest of our inheritance until the redemption of the purchased possession, unto the praise of his glory (Eph. 1:13–14).

You:

- I just want you to know, my friend, the moment you invited Christ into your life, you were saved. God guarantees that one day, you will be with him in heaven.
- Most Christians have experienced the fears you have. But you must move past these fears so you can grow in your faith. You may find it helps to strengthen your faith by reading your Bible, praying, and spending time with other believers.
- Let me help you get started. May I pick you up for church next Sunday?

Additional comment: See objection/responses "How do I know I have enough faith?" and "I've tried it and it didn't work out" in this appendix or chapter 8.

20. I've always believed in God.

Read: "Thou believest that there is one God; thou doest well: the devils also believe, and tremble" (James 2:19).

You:

- I'm glad you believe in God. That's wonderful. But so does the devil. In fact he's even seen God. How are you any different?
- Would you like to receive Jesus as your Savior?

21. I've done too many bad things.

Additional comment: See objection/responses "I'm not good enough" or" God cannot forgive me" in this appendix or chapter 8.

22. I've tried it and it didn't work out.

You:

- Tried what?
- *(If your friend says something like, "I tried that prayer once, and nothing happened")* Apparently that's true. Did you mean the prayer when you said it?
- *(Usually he's not 100 percent sure.)* Tell me about that moment you gave your life to Christ.
- *(Does his testimony make sense; does it sound true?)* Let's take a minute and review the Scriptures. Read them aloud, then tell me what they mean.
- *(If his testimony does not sound true)* If you never found a desire to read your Bible or fellowship with other believers, there is a possibility you were never born again.
- Would you like to make sure?
- *(If he says yes)* Let's review the Scriptures to help you have a better understanding of the gospel. *(Show him the seven "Share Jesus Scriptures" and lead him in prayer.)*

Additional comment: See "How do I know I have enough faith?" or " I'm not sure I'm saved" in this appendix or chapter 8.

23. My beliefs are private.

You:

- Why?
- If what you believe is not true, would you want to know? May I share some Scriptures with you?

Additional comment: You are trying to get at his real objection. Chances are, he has been hurt by a Christian in the past. If he tells you of a bad experience with a Christian who tried to witness to him, see the objection "A Christian hurt me" in this appendix or chapter 8.

24. My friends will think I'm crazy if I accept Jesus.

You:
- Why?
- If they are really your friends, won't they be happy and thrilled that the God of the universe lives inside of you and that all of your sins are forgiven? After all, when they see you change, they may want what you have.

Read: "Likewise, I say unto you, there is joy in the presence of the angels of God over one sinner that repenteth" (Luke 15:10).

You: Are you ready?

25. The argument never stops.

You:
- Why are you angry?
- Why does the presentation of the gospel make you hostile?
- If for some reason you found out everything I've said about the gospel and about Jesus is true, what would you do about it?
- *(If he says he will not believe)* Why? *(otherwise)* That's wonderful, because I was the same way. *(You may want to give him a short testimony of how Jesus changed your life.)*
- *(Try to get him to open up with one or more of the following questions:)* I was pretty open with you about my life. What was the most traumatic thing that has ever happened to you? Do you have a fear? Are you afraid of death? Did your parents ever hurt you? Would accepting God's love scare you to death? Has anyone ever loved you? Do you ever feel alone?

- Would you like to accept Jesus as your Savior?

Additional comment: Do not feel like a failure if he does not respond. Keep praying for him.

26. The church only wants my money.

You:

- Has the church ever asked you for money? It's true that most churches take an offering. But it is usually the members who are expected to give, not the visitors.
- God doesn't want your money. But when you become a believer, something happens to your heart. You give because you want to. If you don't give in joy, you shouldn't give at all.
- The church doesn't want your money; the church wants you to surrender your life to Jesus. Are you willing to do that?

27. There are many paths to God.

You: You are correct, all roads lead to God. But here's the problem, what are you going to say when you get there? For God is either going to meet you as your Savior or as your judge.

Read: "That at the name of Jesus every knee should bow, of things in heaven, and things in earth, and things under the earth; And that every tongue should confess that Jesus Christ is Lord, to the glory of God the Father" (Phil. 2:10–11).

You: Are you ready to invite Christ into your heart?

Additional comment: See objection/responses "Cults are the answer?" "I'm a member of another world religion," "I'm God," "There are many religions in the world," "I'm not good enough," and "I don't believe in truth" in this appendix or chapter 8.

28. There are many religions in the world.

You:

- I've discovered all of the religions in the world can be divided into two groups. Imagine, every religion other than Christianity is in my left hand—Mormonism, Buddhism, Hinduism, Judaism, whatever "ism,"—and Christianity is in my right hand. Everyone in my left hand makes two distinctive claims: (a) Jesus is not God, or he is not the only God. He may be a great prophet, teacher, or good man, but not the Messiah; and (b) If you do enough good works through your own efforts, such as terrorists acts, diet, or good deeds, you can receive some form of salvation.
- Two opposite claims cannot possibly be true. I would be willing to admit that if the "ism" pile is true, my faith would be in vain. Would you be willing to admit, if the Christianity in my right hand is true, that your faith is in vain? Let's examine the evidence so we can find out which one of us is possibly in error.
- Christianity claims that Jesus is God and that God has come to us in Jesus who lived, died on the cross, and rose from the grave that we might have eternal life. Christianity claims:

Read: "For by grace are ye saved through faith; and that not of yourselves: it is the gift of God: Not of works, lest any man should boast" (Eph. 2:8–9).

You:

- Can both of these teachings be true?
- May I show you some Scriptures that changed my life?

Additional comment: See objection/responses "Cults are the answer?" "There are many religions in the world," "There are many paths to God," "I'm a member of another world religion," "I'm Jewish," and "How can I know the Bible is true?" in this appendix or chapter 8.

29. There are many translations of the Bible.

You:
- You are correct. Did you know they all say the same thing?
- Let's turns to Romans 3:23.

Additional comment: This objection usually appears only at the beginning of the "Share Jesus Presentation."

30. There are too many errors in the Bible.

You: *(Don't go off on a rabbit trail. Instead, with all the love you can muster, hand your friend your Bible.)* Would you show me one?

Friend: Well, I can't.

You: I can't either. Let's turn to Romans 3:23.

Additional comment: See objection/response "How can I know the Bible is true?" in this appendix or chapter 8.

31. There are too many hypocrites in the church.

You:
- You are absolutely correct. There are hypocrites in every church. I'm so glad you are concerned about that, because, sir, when you join the perfect church, it won't be perfect any longer.
- Jesus said not to follow hypocrites, but to follow him.

- I'm glad you know the difference between a hypocrite and a genuine person.
- *(Smile.)* If you accept Christ as your Savior and I see you begin to act like a hypocrite, I will remind you of this conversation.
- Are you ready to pray?

Note: Some of your friends may want to discuss dishonest TV evangelists or others who misrepresent Christ. In this event,

You: If I falsely represented myself to you as a realtor in order to scam your money, does that mean all realtors are dishonest? Of course not. Just because a person says he represents Christ does not mean he is a representative of Christ. Only Christ knows his heart. Would you let a dishonest person stand in your way of knowing God's love for you? Are you ready to pray?

32. What about my family?

You: What about your family?

Read: "He that loveth father or mother more than me is not worthy of me: and he that loveth son or daughter more than me is not worthy of me. And he that taketh not his cross, and followeth after me, is not worthy of me" (Matt. 10:37–38).

You: What does this say to you?

Read: "Suppose ye that I am come to give peace on earth? I tell you, Nay; but rather division: For from henceforth there shall be five in one house divided, three against two, and two against three. The father shall be divided against the son, and the son against the father; the mother against the daughter, and the daughter against the mother; the mother in law against her daughter in law, and the daughter in law against her mother in law" (Luke 12:51–53).

You:
- What does this say to you?
- Are you ready to pray?

33. What about those who never hear the gospel?

You:
- That's not you, is it?
- What does the Bible say will happen to those who have heard and have not responded?
- You've heard the gospel. Will you respond?

Additional comment: You may want to have your friend read the following verse aloud: "For the invisible things of him from the creation of the world are clearly seen, being understood by the things that are made, even his eternal power and Godhead; so that they are without excuse" (Rom. 1:20).

34. Why does God let bad things happen?

Note: Allow this person to vent if he wants. Your job is to listen. When he is done,

You:
- What about you? Who taught you to tell your first lie?
- Let me tell you the story about Adam and Eve in the garden of Eden. Before they disobeyed God, the garden was perfect. There was no evil because there was no sin. When Adam and Eve disobeyed God by eating the fruit God forbade them to eat, sin entered the world and into us. That is why no one has to be taught to lie, cheat, steal, or lust or

to be envious of other people. It is part of the nature that is in us.

- Jesus has made a difference in my life. He has forgiven me and taught me to base my choices on his goodness. Would you like to know his forgiveness too?

Note: If your friend is dealing with a tragedy that has happened to him, continue:

You: You may wonder why God allowed that to happen to you. But here are your choices. You can walk through the rest of your life alone in your pain, or you can choose to hold onto a nail-scarred hand. What do you want to do?

35. You can't possibly know what truth is.

You: Why?

Note: In this object lesson, which you act out with your friend, keep the mood friendly. As nicely as possible,

You:
- May I borrow your watch? *(You may use other jewelry or a credit card.)* Put the watch in your pocket. When he asks for it back, smile.
- No, my truth is taking watches from people who don't believe in truth. *(When he protests, ask,)*
- Why is it wrong to steal?
- As you listen, smile and give the watch back. *(He will probably say, "It just is.")* How do you know? You just told me that there are no rights or wrongs. How can it be wrong if I steal your watch?
- I'll tell you how I know it's wrong. Because God says so. See, you cannot hide behind the statement

that there is no truth. May I show you some verses of Scripture that have had a major impact on my life?

36. You must think you are better than me.

You:

- I am not better then you; I am simply better off.
- Like you, I have broken God's commandments and laws and was condemned to hell. But by his grace and unfailing love, God sent someone into my life to tell me about Jesus. That made me realize how dirty I was in the presence of a holy God.
- I asked God to forgive me, and he did. It doesn't make me better than you; it makes me forgiven.
- Now I am giving you the same opportunity someone gave me.
- Would you like to be forgiven and know what it is like to be born again and have a personal relationship with Jesus Christ?

Appendix 3 ASSIGNMENT

Your assignment is to share the first five questions with at least one person this week. Pray for God's leading. Watch for opportunities. Call those whom God has placed on your heart. If you need a warm-up, practice the questions on a friend, or say them out loud to yourself. Be obedient to God's call and share Jesus without fear.

- I will no longer be a silent Christian.
- I will continually look for those with whom you are working so I can share Jesus with them.
- Since I understand Christ's resurrection power lives in me and I lack nothing to keep my Lord's Great Commission, I will obey that command to go and make disciples.
- I will live my life so that Philemon verse 6 will be actively demonstrated, allowing you to fulfill your promises in my life.

"That the communication of thy faith may become effectual by the acknowledging of every good thing which is in you in Christ Jesus" (Philem. v. 6).

Signed:______________________________ Date:_____________

Appendix 4
BILL FAY'S TESTIMONY

My life began in an upper middle-class family. My father was vice president of a company called General Foods and introduced a line of frozen foods called Birds Eye.

Meanwhile, I was raised with the classic silver spoon in my mouth. My biggest concern as a young adult was trying to get to my father's money before he blew it. I wasn't fast enough. I watched my father die destitute in a veterans' hospital without a penny to his name.

I decided this was not going to happen to me. I would be number one and secure the things the world could give, regardless of the cost.

At age sixteen, I got a girl pregnant and got married. I soon headed off to college where I learned a few things that weren't the norm. For instance, my study habits became easier when I learned the mimeograph room often had the tests before the teachers did. I also met a man who taught me how to become a professional gambler and card cheat. I began to put myself through college by taking money with my deck of fifty-two.

Upon graduation, I divorced my wife, advanced my career, and found another woman to marry. She was a very nice, kind woman who allowed me to do whatever I wanted, whenever I wanted.

When I was twenty-two, I was hired by an Atlanta corporation. I was determined to be number one in everything I did. I was the number-one salesman, the number-one district manager, and ready to become the number-one regional manager.

I loved golf because it allowed me an opportunity to hustle the members of the country club at the famous nineteenth hole, where my deck of cards was loaded. I easily paid the golf club's fifteen thousand initiation fee by cheating those foolish enough to play gin rummy with me.

My life began to accelerate in its craziness. Because of my reputation as a gambler, I was invited to go to Las Vegas as a guest. When I arrived there, I was impressed by the power, the limousines, the fountain in the middle of my suite, the flashy women, and the endless supply of money. I thought to myself, *If I can just get connected into all this, my life will be fine.*

One evening, I went to the baccarat table where the heavy-duty players gambled. I was drawn to this table because they used cash instead of chips, and it was not unusual for the table to be piled with millions of dollars.

One day, I watched a man who kept losing and losing and losing. He lost $200,000 in twenty minutes. I had finished a couple of drinks, and I turned to him and said, "You really don't know what you're doing, do you?"

He replied, "Wise guy, if you're so smart, why don't you show me?"

He invited me across the street to Caesars Palace. When I walked into Caesars with him, I could tell people knew him. The blackjack dealers glanced up, and crowds parted as he walked to the baccarat table. He whispered into the croupier's ear, and he cleared the table and removed the gambling limit. He ordered fifty thousand dollars as comfortably as you might order a glass of milk and handed the money to me. He said, "Play, wise guy."

I hit a hot streak. In about fifteen minutes, I had won back a little over a quarter of a million dollars. This man not only became my friend; he became my godfather. I became connected with the Mafia—the underworld—the syndicate—and began to wholesale Mafia money around the country.

Despite my illegal connections, I kept my corporate life going—achievement after achievement, promotion after promotion. I was now the manager of a major corporation in Houston. I was so crazy that one day, when I was on the phone talking to a woman in Kansas City, I asked her, "What do you look like?"

She told me she was attractive, and I asked, "What do you want out of life?"

When she said, "Power and money," I was on the next plane to meet her. I took her to dinner and suggested, "Let's get married."

I went back home to my wife of twelve years to inform her I was leaving. Then I got into my Cadillac, drove to Kansas City, picked up this woman, then drove to Denver to become the new chief executive officer of a multimillion-dollar, multi-international corporation.

One afternoon, I stood in my office and stared at my mahogany desk. My chauffeur-driven limousine was outside. I had an unlimited expense account, diamond rings, Rolexes, and gold jewelry. I thought, *What's next? I have both legal and illegal money. I have power, both corporately and illegally. Yet something is missing.*

I dismissed the thought. I couldn't afford to think that way for long. I continued in my goal to become a nationally ranked racquetball player and came close to succeeding. Yet no matter what I did, I found it was fun for only a while.

No one ever knew how lonely I really was. My third wife decided to leave me for another man. It was only by God's grace I did not put a contract on her to have her killed.

It was then I met my current wife, Peggy. As we started to date, I decided to build a new, but unusual, enterprise. Because I understood the loneliness of men's lives, I built Fantasy Island in Lakewood, Colorado. Fantasy Island became one of the largest houses of prostitution in the United States.

One day, I took Peggy to Las Vegas to show her how people would cater to my every whim. Ironically, while we were at the same baccarat table where the insanity had begun so many years earlier, my attorney called. He said, "There's a warrant out for your arrest."

My reaction was, "For what? I haven't done anything."

He said, "They've raided the house of prostitution. It's all over the news."

I was aghast. "Why?"

I flew back to get arrested and received probation. All that meant to me was "Don't get caught again."

My hands were clean, but my heart was unchanged. I knew if I got caught for anything, I'd be off to prison for six to eight years. But I was still willing to make any deal, providing it was sweet enough.

My corporation didn't like its chief executive officer making national newspapers every day for a week, so the management fired me. I was undaunted and got in the executive search business and started to make top dollars again. So in many regards, I was still the winner, yet somehow I did not feel OK.

Over the years, I had looked for peace. Somehow, by God's providence, I had found peace in a place called Lost Valley Ranch. It sits on about eighty-five hundred acres of Colorado mountain country. Every time I went there, I felt great. Then, when I'd leave to return to my life of madness, reality would hit. Driving toward home, I would get an acid burn in my stomach and tears in my eyes. I couldn't understand why leaving was so difficult. One day I figured it out. I realized the whole ranch was loaded with "Christians." I got so I could spot them. They had this funny little look in their eyes, and if I aggravated them, they would quote Scriptures at me.

One Easter Sunday while I was at the ranch, I decided to do what many non-Christians do on Easter Sunday—I went to church. I rode my horse out on the meadow and heard a young man named Bob Foster preach a sermon I'll never forget. He said, "There's a difference between 'happiness' and 'inner peace.' Happiness is like the smell of a new car, a new dating relationship, closing a big business deal, illicit drugs, or sex. You get high. You're 'happy,' but it never lasts." He added, "Some highs are higher than other highs. Some highs last different lengths of time, but they always end."

I thought to myself, *The kid is right. That's my life—achieve, get, do, be, then . . . nothing.*

Bob explained, "Inner peace is different."

His words struck me. I knew I didn't have inner peace, and I wondered how to get it.

He continued, "You'll find inner peace only with a personal relationship with Christ."

I thought, *Oh, give me a break.*

I got on my horse, rode out of the meadow, and drove back to Denver.

For the next year, off and on, Christians came into my life to tell me about the person of Jesus Christ. When they did, they were insulted, persecuted, and antagonized. Many of them walked away, believing they'd failed. But I never forgot the name, the face, the words, or any one of them who told me about the Lord Jesus.

Then God sent Paul and Kathie Grant into my life. Paul, a Jewish believer in Christ, was sitting at home one morning, praying, "Lord, I want to go to the racquetball court today and share my faith."

Later, I pushed open the door of the racquetball court and saw him. I blurted, "What are you doing here on Yom Kippur? Why aren't you out doing whatever you Jews do on holidays?"

He replied, "I am also a Christian. Yom Kippur is the day Jews ask God to forgive them of their sins for another year. I don't have to do that because I've already received forgiveness through Jesus, the Messiah."

"Oh, please, give me a break," I sneered.

For months afterward, Dr. Grant would stand by his locker while I asked questions, deliberately trying to make him late. I thought, *What a stupid fool! How can this idiot sit here and let me do this to him when he has a waiting room full of patients?*

Yet Paul was my first true friend. He called after I'd been arrested for the raid on my house of prostitution. Now, I had received hundreds of phone calls—calls from attorneys wondering if their clients' names were found in the records and calls from men who were still wondering where the girls were. Yet Paul's call was different. He asked, "Are you OK?"

That question went through me like a shot. He followed it by asking, "Would you consider coming to church with Kathie and me?" I turned to Peggy and said, "We'll go, but whatever you do, don't sign anything."

At the church service, I listened to this guy talk like he was never going to quit. Afterward, I recognized a man in the congregation whom I had given a brochure for Fantasy Island. When I had asked him if he'd like to be my guest, he'd said, "That's not part of my life." His response had made an impression, and even though the incident had happened years ago, I hadn't forgotten.

Afterward, Paul and Kathie took Peggy and me back to their home and gave us what was the first Christian testimony I'd ever heard. Kathie looked so pure as she radiated her personal relationship with Jesus that I thought, *I wonder if she's ever had a zit?*

When she set a pot of tea in front of me, I got nervous. I was into bookmaking and had some $100,000 in bets on the day's sporting events. The last thing I wanted was to be delayed from the TV by a pot of tea.

Then Kathie shared her life. She talked about the times she had been sexually molested, how she had been a mistress to a man called "the king of oil" in Indonesia, and how she attempted to take her own life on four different occasions.

I sat there, not believing a word she said. I felt she had made up every bit of it just to hook me into joining her cult. As we left, I told Peggy, "That is fine for them, but let's you and me go home and have a drink."

Unknown to me, the Lakewood Police Department in Colorado had decided justice had not been served. One night, the police sent out an attractive police woman, undercover. She offered to sell me a stolen television, implying she came with it. I gave her $200 and was arrested. My bond was $250,000. Because the police pulled the sting on a Friday night, I had to spend the weekend in jail.

Monday, when I was released, a sense of panic hit me. I realized I had violated my probationary terms. I would go to prison for the next six to eight years.

I remember sitting at my kitchen table crying crocodile tears, not because I was repentant, but because I was panicked. I tried to think of a way out. I thought of drugs and alcohol, but I didn't want more problems in my life. I considered the idea of escape, and at that time I had money to run. I even contemplated suicide. But by God's grace, I didn't take that route.

That's when God used my unbelieving wife. She said, "Why don't we call the man who married us?"

I snapped at her. "I don't want that stuff in my life!"

But the Holy Spirit is more powerful than my ignorance. Later, I called that pastor. Through my tears, I said, "I want inner peace in my life."

The next day, I drove eighty-five miles to his little country church. When I walked in, the church didn't even have a rug on the dusty floor. But, in a matter of moments, the floor held a puddle of my tears. At 10:00 A.M. on March 4, 1981, I found out what it meant to know and to meet Jesus Christ as both my Lord and my Savior.

God chose to take my life and flip it. The first evidence of what was to come happened on my drive down the mountain. I had the first unselfish thought I had ever had in my entire life. I began to remember the daughter I had abandoned so many years earlier. For the first time I wondered, *Where's Tammy?*

When I got home I found evidence of God's perfect timing. Although I had not heard from Tammy in twenty-three years, she had left a message on my answering machine. She said a strange thing for a daughter to say to her own dad. She said, "I saw your name in the newspapers from all your arrests, and I would like to meet you."

A short while later, I met my daughter and asked her to forgive me. Then I had the greatest privilege I have ever had in my entire life. I held my daughter's hand while she surrendered her heart and her life to Jesus Christ.

Although I fully expected to go to prison, God had other plans. Even though my Mafia attorney never showed up for my day in court and my local attorney subpoenaed all the wrong people, a miracle took place. Not only did the judge dismiss my case; he barred it from further prosecution at the district level. I walked out of the court that day, free to the world, but more importantly, Christ had freed me from my sins.

For two years afterward, I prayed for an opportunity to go back to the Lakewood Police Department and let the police know Christ had changed my life. One day, the assistant chief of police was having lunch when my name came up. He pushed back his chair and said, "Even God can't forgive that man."

Someone said, "Why don't you find out for yourself?"

I'll never forget the day I met him for lunch. He walked in and said, "I came to find out if what you have found is truth in your life." Then he said, "When I told people at the department that I was going to meet with you, one detective offered to wire me and another offered to cover me."

That day, I held the hand of the man who orchestrated both my arrests and we prayed together. Three months later, he introduced me to the policewoman, a dedicated Christian, who had arrested me and put me in the back of her car. Only this time, we went to church together. She has become one of my closest Christian friends.

If God can change my life, he can change yours. There are five simple steps to knowing Jesus Christ:

1. Admit to God you are a sinner.
2. Want forgiveness for your sin.
3. Believe in your heart that Jesus Christ died on the cross for you and rose again.
4. Be willing to surrender your life to Jesus Christ.
5. Receive Jesus Christ as your Lord and your Savior.

To receive him, pray this prayer by simply reading these words to God: "Heavenly Father, I am a sinner. I want forgiveness for all of my sins. Father, I believe in my heart that Jesus

Christ died on the cross for me and rose again. I give you my life to do with as you wish. If I've been walking astray from your Word and your will, I come back to begin again. Father, I want Jesus to come into my life. Fill me with you, Father. Come into my life, come into my heart, Lord Jesus. I love you. I ask this in Christ's name. Amen."

If you have prayed to receive Christ, I want to welcome you to the eternal kingdom of Jesus. Tell someone about your new commitment. It is important to find and attend a Christ-centered church that believes and teaches the Bible.

God bless you as you continue your journey with him.

ENDNOTES

Chapter 3

1. Michael P. Green (ed.), *Illustrations for Biblical Preaching* (Grand Rapids, Mich.: Baker Book House, 1990).

Chapter 6

1. John D. Woodbridge (gen. ed.), *More Than Conquerors* (Chicago, Ill.: The Moody Bible Institute of Chicago, 1992), pp. 145–46.

Chapter 8

1. Ripley Entertainment, *Ripley's Believe It or Not! Strange Coincidences* (New York: Tom Doherry Associates, 1990).
2. Josh McDowell, *More Than a Carpenter* (Wheaton, Ill.: Tyndale House Publishers, Inc., 1977).
3. Ibid.

Chapter 10

1. Jim Cymbala, *Fresh Wind, Fresh Fire* (Grand Rapids, Mich.: Zondervan Publishing House, 1997), pp. 24, 25, 27.
2. Kathleen G. Grant, *The Key to His Kingdom: Praying in the Word of God* (P.O. Box 6001, Littleton, Colo. 80121), pp. 94, 95, 97–101, 103. The Bread of Life Foundation (1995), 303-781-6484, fax: 303-781-6585; used with permission.

Chapter 11

1. Lee Strobel, *Inside the Mind of Unchurched Harry and Mary: How to Reach Friends and Family Who Avoid God and the Church* (Grand Rapids, Mich.: Zondervan Publishing House, 1993), p. 83.

ABOUT THE AUTHORS

William Fay

Bill, a 1987 graduate of Denver Seminary, has shared his faith with more than twenty-five thousand people on a one-to-one basis. Since 1981, he has taught his no-argument approach to witnessing in churches around the world, prompting 30 to 100 percent of his listeners to share their faith within the following week.

Bill has written the series *Share Jesus without Fear* for LifeWay Christian Resources and has inspired the notes in the *Share Jesus without Fear New Testament*. His pamphlet *How to Share Your Faith without an Argument* has 3.5 million copies in print. His radio program *Let's Go with Bill Fay* is now heard on more than one hundred radio stations from Nome, Alaska, to Valdosta, Georgia.

Linda Evans Shepherd

Linda is an award-winning author. Her latest books include *Encouraging Hands—Encouraging Hearts: How to Be a Good Friend*

(Servant) and *Heart-Stirring Stories of Romance* and *Heart-Stirring Stories of Love* (Broadman & Holman, 2000).

She is a nationally known speaker and member of the National Speaker's Association.